God's

**Understanding Israel
and End-time Revival**

TSUNAMI

Peter Tsukahira

Bridge-Logos

Alachua, Florida 32615

Bridge-Logos

Alachua, FL 32615USA

God's Tsunami—Understanding Israel and End-time Revival
by Peter Tsukahira

Website: www.Gods-Tsunami.com E-mail: info@Gods-Tsunami.com

Library of Congress Catalog Card Number: 2009923611
International Standard Book Number 978-0-88270-9840

G163.316.N.m903.35230

Dedication

THIS BOOK IS DEDICATED to Derek Prince who has been an example to me since I became a believer in the early 1970s. His life and Bible teaching set a standard for so many around the world. We became friends in 2000, when he came to teach on prophecy at our School of Ministry on Mt. Carmel in Israel. I was honored that he read the manuscript for *God's Tsunami*, commented on it, and wrote an endorsement just three months before he went to be with the Lord on September 24, 2003. All who knew him will miss this great teacher and servant of God.

Acknowledgments

I AM INDEBTED to those friends and co-workers who offered suggestions, contributed biblical insights, and prayed for me and this project. To Rita, my wife, and Eden and Daniel, our children, my abiding love and appreciation. My prayer is that God will use these teachings to bless and build up His people.

Peter Tsukahira
Mt. Carmel

Table of Contents

Preface to the New Edition

GOD'S TSUNAMI WAS ORIGINALLY PUBLISHED in 2003. As this book was being prepared for its second printing in December 2004, a massive earthquake followed by huge tsunamis struck Southeast Asia. They brought death and destruction on a scale beyond any natural disaster the modern world had known. In a matter of hours, more than two hundred thousand people perished. Our minds could not begin to comprehend the human pain and suffering that was caused by the onslaught of those giant waves. We grieved for the thousands who died in this tragedy and for the losses experienced by so many. At the time, CNN's Asia Bureau Chief, Mike Chinnoy, called the tsunami a "disaster of almost biblical proportions."

Although it was written in the same general time frame, the subject of *God's Tsunami* is not the great natural disaster in Asia. This book is about a tsunami that is taking place in the spiritual realm. There are, however, clear parallels between the spiritual and the physical. A tsunami is caused by highly concentrated pulses of energy released by an undersea earthquake. This energy travels through the ocean at close to five-hundred-miles-per-hour—the speed of a modern jet airliner. It becomes a powerful wave when it enters shallow coastal water. We saw how these waves can permanently change the shape of entire regions in an instant.

This book describes how God is releasing unprecedented power through the gospel today and particularly in Asia. The release of God's power is often unseen on the surface of human society, but when it comes into view, the effects are profound. Whole nations can be transformed. We know from the Bible that when God's kingdom advances on Earth there is a clash of spiritual forces. Events surrounding the recent tsunamis show that the depths of the Earth are being stirred and spiritual powers and principalities challenged as God moves the world into His final harvest.

Author's Note

This book is written with the understanding that the Bible from Genesis to Revelation is God's Word and inspired by the Holy Spirit. No other source or tradition can equal its authority. I have chosen to quote most Scriptures from the New King James Version of the Bible because of its readability in the English language. The Bible verses quoted are integral to the message of the book. I hope that even the most familiar ones will be read. Bold type has been used to emphasize significant words or phrases.

Introduction

WHEN THE GULF WAR BEGAN in January 1991, my family and I had been living in Israel for three years. In the months leading up to the war, Saddam Hussein had promised to "burn half of Israel" with missiles possibly loaded with weapons of mass destruction. After the first day of allied bombing in Baghdad, Iraqi missiles began landing in Israeli cities. In the following weeks, missile strikes within Israel became an almost regular occurrence. I remember one evening attack with clarity. The urgent moan of the air raid sirens seemed to echo all over our port city of Haifa. It was early evening, but already the streets were strangely empty and silent. Almost everyone was indoors in expectation of an attack. It felt like a scene from a movie that could have been titled *The End of the World*. We made our way into the sealed room—one of our bedrooms where the window was sealed with plastic sheets and cracks around the door were covered with packing tape. I helped my wife, Rita, put our one-year-old son into his tent-like breathing apparatus, and then I checked on our five-and-a-half-year-old daughter to see that her gas mask was on securely. She smiled at me through the eyepieces of the almost comically grotesque black rubber mask. We put on our own masks and checked to see that the boxes still contained the spring-loaded, nerve gas antidote syringes.

From the time of the siren, we knew that we had two minutes to get into our sealed room and put on our gas masks before the Iraqi SCUD missiles could be expected to hit. If the missiles were targeted for our city, we would hear the roar of the Patriot anti-missile missiles taking off to try to intercept the incoming SCUDs. On this particular evening, we heard the Patriot missiles and then *BOOM!*, the house shook. The entire building seemed to shift around us, and the windows rattled. It felt and sounded like a missile had exploded right in our neighborhood.

"Get down on the floor!" I yelled, and we crouched on the floor tiles. Rita was frantically trying to move our son's tent onto the floor. In an instant, everything was silent. We asked ourselves, "Was it a nerve gas warhead?" We wouldn't know if we were safe until an "All Clear" was broadcast by radio or television. We had to stay in the room with our gas masks on and wait.

During the 1991 Gulf War, we lived in an apartment on Mount Carmel in Haifa. Nine of the thirty-nine missiles launched at Israel came into our city. The one that shook our home detonated in the air less than one kilometer from our neighborhood. Dozens of houses lost their windows. The twisted, smoking wreckage of the missile landed in a nearby valley where it burned away the underbrush and lay smoldering for hours. Miraculously, no one in Haifa was hurt, and none of the missiles carried nerve gas warheads. The war ended on the Jewish holiday of Purim, when the Book of Esther is read in the synagogues. The nation had literally been shaken, but we joyfully gave thanks to God for extending His hand of protection once more over the house of Israel.

I am an Asian-American Israeli, and I have lived my life between three very different nations. The first nation is the United States, the world's dominant economy and culture. The second is Japan, a nation that is rich in its blending of ancient and modern Asian traditions. The third nation is Israel, a newborn, modern society with a unique heritage of centuries-old biblical culture. The principles that I have learned and now teach have come from serving God while living between these three divergent and dynamic worlds.

My grandparents immigrated to the United States from Japan about one hundred years ago. My mother and father were born in California. They were part of the generation of Japanese-Americans that were sent from their homes on the west coast of the United States and relocated in camps by the U.S. government for the duration of World War II. While their families were in the camps, my father taught Japanese to American soldiers. After the war, my father completed his doctoral studies in Asian History at Harvard University. I was born in Boston during those post-war baby boom years.

When I was ten, my father was working for the U.S. Department of State, and he received an assignment to serve in the U.S. Embassy in Tokyo. I spent my teenage years attending an international school in Japan, and then I returned to the Boston area for university. America was still struggling with the Vietnam War, the Civil Rights Movement, and a youth-oriented cultural revolution that was sweeping the nation. I became caught up in this turbulent vortex, and I didn't emerge until my best friend committed suicide. His death triggered a search for truth in me. That search led my Jewish girlfriend, Rita, and me into the mountains of the American West. Several months after my friend's death, Rita visited a coffeehouse ministry called "Shalom" in Santa Fe, New Mexico. There she heard another young Jewish hippie tell about his encounter with Jesus as his Messiah and the change that had come to his life. That same night a deep change took place in Rita's heart, and she also came to believe in Jesus as the Messiah. I could not deny the obvious, immediate, and radical transformation that had happened in her life. My own questioning ended soon after that when I prayed to become God's servant, and discovered that Jesus is God's Son and the Savior of the world.

This discovery changed the direction of our lives and, soon after, Rita and I were married. My desire to be involved in ministry led me to enroll in a Bible school and then in seminary. I also began to work in the computer industry. These dual streams took us to Japan in the 1980s, where I served as associate pastor of a growing international fellowship in Tokyo for over five years. I also worked in the Japanese computer industry, and Rita taught in a university. We knew even then that one day we would live and work in the land of Israel. In 1987, doors opened for us, and we moved to Israel with our two-year-old daughter. Because Rita is from a Jewish family, we were invited to come as new immigrants and to become citizens of this newly re-created nation. We joined the more than three million immigrants who have come from over 120 other countries to populate this land since the founding of the modern state in 1948. We settled in the city of Haifa, which is built on Mount Carmel, the location of the prophet Elijah's confrontation with the false prophets of Baal. Our son was born in Haifa in 1989.

We came to Haifa with a vision to see a congregation established that would be of benefit to both Jews and Gentiles. We began to gather for fellowship and prayer with a handful of other believers living near our home. In 1990, we met David and Karen Davis, also new immigrants. They were moving from Jerusalem to Haifa to start a rehabilitation center for drug addicts called *Beit Nitzachon* (House of Victory). After the Gulf War in 1991, the Davises invited us to join them in co-founding a congregation that began at the rehabilitation center where they lived. The congregation became known as *Kehilat HaCarmel* (Carmel Assembly). One of the foundational visions of this congregation is the *One New Man* of Jews, Arabs, and other Gentiles worshipping together in the unity of the Holy Spirit.

Over the years, we have been privileged to participate in the return of the Jewish people to the land of their inheritance and the re-emergence of an indigenous Israeli Messianic body. In the last few years we have seen dozens of Israeli Jews come to faith in their Messiah. For the first time in nearly 2000 years, voices proclaiming, "*Yeshua hu Adon,*" ("Jesus is Lord") can be heard in congregations throughout the country. Since we have been living in Israel, over one million new immigrants have arrived from the former Soviet Union. In a country of just six million Jewish and Arab citizens, absorption of over a million newcomers in such a short time has been quite a challenge. Today, more than 20 percent of the Jewish population are new immigrants from the former Soviet Union, and every major city has Russian-language newspapers, television channels, and radio broadcasts. In addition, there is a remarkable openness to the gospel among these Russian-speaking immigrants.

Soon after our congregation was established, our friends Eitan and Connie came to live in Haifa. Eitan was the young man that Rita heard in Santa Fe as he testified of his faith in Jesus. Eitan and his family joined our congregation and he served on the leadership team. Later, with our blessing, he and several other immigrant families began their own congregation named *Ohalei Rachamim* (Tents of Mercy) in a suburb of Haifa. Almost from the beginning, their congregation faced a series of intense challenges including various forms of harassment and the fire bombing of their sanctuary. They continued conducting their services in both Hebrew and Russian, and now they have built a strong and vibrant community. Recently, Tents of Mercy launched their own daughter congregation in another part of the city. God is clearly doing a new thing in our region, and the largest numbers of new believers are among these immigrants who have come to Israel searching for spiritual truth.

Looking back over the years, I can see that we as a family have been riding a powerful wave of God's purposes from our starting point in North America, moving westward to Japan, and then even further west to the land of Israel, the furthest edge of Asia. We have made a life-long commitment to this nation and its people, both Jews and Arabs. We have learned that Jesus, the Prince of Peace, is the only Ruler who can bring lasting peace to the Middle East. Jesus said that His kingdom is "not of this world," but this kingdom has the power to change lives. In our journey, we have discovered a spiritual home in the culture of God's kingdom. This home is "… *the city which has foundations, whose builder and maker is God*" (Hebrews 11:10).

Chapter 1

God Is Shaking the Earth

For thus says the LORD of hosts: "Once more (it is a little while) I will shake heaven and earth, the sea and dry land; and I will shake all nations, and they shall come to the Desire of All Nations, and I will fill this temple with glory," says the LORD of hosts (Haggai 2:6-7).

A TSUNAMI IS A MASSIVE TIDAL WAVE in the ocean that is caused by an underwater earthquake. Earthquakes often occur at fault lines or places where giant sections of the Earth's crust push and grind against each other. Today, God is shaking the Earth, and a major spiritual fault line runs through the nation of Israel. It is here that ancient spiritual powers and dark principalities are colliding. Shock waves in the spiritual realm are expanding outwardly toward every nation and impacting political, economic, and cultural realms across the planet. Stirred and accelerated by these deep tremors, a tsunami of revival is racing across the globe. Crisis and great change can be expected wherever this tsunami flows. It rearranges the status quo, tearing down old traditions and launching new movements of

God's Spirit in places where biblical faith has never been seen. People of vision are able to see this wave coming. Some will catch it and surf its mighty currents. Great ministries will be born suddenly—in the blink of an eye, while others will be bypassed and left stranded on suddenly unfamiliar landscapes. A generation of great change has come. God is shaking the heavens and the Earth again today.

This book was written in order to bring revelation rather than simply explanation to the reader. Its aim is not to instruct academically, but to provide prophetic insight by illuminating selected facts that lie where history and biblical prophecy meet. The purpose of revelation is to equip leaders to understand the times in which they live based on God's viewpoint. By revelation, God's Word becomes a lens through which we can evaluate the importance and timing of key events that mold the contours of our world and impact our daily lives.

Revelation is closely connected to faith since our beliefs reflect the way we see and understand the world in which we live. Our beliefs form the basis of the way we approach life. The insight of revelation is meant to touch us at the level of our beliefs. This is at a level more profound than knowledge, more powerful than human instinct, and deeper than culture. Someone once said, "Truth about God is caught, not taught." This means that important truths about God are spiritually revealed rather than learned intellectually.

What God is doing in the world today has important aspects that are universal, as well as others that are particular to a certain people, time, and place. To paraphrase another writer, "God thinks globally and acts locally." When we are facing challenges in our immediate surroundings it is difficult to put the whole picture together. Moreover, the prophetic significance of God's actions is often obscured by the news media's tendency to view any international event through the eyes of politics. Like a giant jigsaw puzzle, the full picture of world events as seen through God's eyes must be assembled by revelation, piece by piece. It can be a frustrating and confusing task unless we begin with pieces that form a reference for the others. Most people put together jigsaw puzzles by beginning with the edges. Today, God's purposes for Israel are like those pieces of the puzzle that provide a reference or frame for the others.

Israel at the Epicenter

Why does Israel, a small Middle Eastern country, command such constant attention in the news media today? It seems that Israel is somehow at the root of the political unrest that is escalating around the world. Israel is ultimately blamed by its enemies for triggering each new act of international terrorism. Certainly Israel, like any other nation, has political adversaries but that does not explain the pervasive anti-Israel sentiment linked to terror attacks in countries thousands of miles from Jerusalem. There must be a spiritual dynamic at work linking these determined acts of murder and suicide. Those responsible for the attacks on the World Trade Center towers in New York and the Pentagon in Washington D.C. on September 11, 2001, were members of Al Qaeda, a group of Islamic radicals who stated that a primary reason for their attack was America's support for Israel. I was in Southeast Asia in October 2002, when a terrorist's bomb demolished a popular nightclub in Bali, Indonesia. Over two hundred people died in the blast, mostly young Australians on holiday. Months later, one of those who plotted the bombing was sentenced to death by a court in Jakarta. After the verdict the *New York Times,* on August 8, 2003, quoted the defendant's lawyer by saying, "He doesn't have anything personal against the Australians. The targets were the Americans and the Jews."

Those who are the enemies of the God of the Bible appear to be using Israel as a scapegoat, a means to advance their own agenda or theology. However, God is not frustrated by human brutality or the cynicism of modern politics. His purposes are still being accomplished in spite of rampant terrorism. He is using tiny Israel to mark a *line in the sand* and to draw all peoples into a valley of decision. God's ultimate desire is to call His elect from every nation into the Kingdom of Heaven. He is requiring the world to make a decision regarding who He is and what He has said in His Word, the Bible. As in the days of old, Israel is again God's instrument—His lever to shake the nations. Some will conclude that Israel merely represents another turn in the political history of the world, and that it has no divine right to exist. Others will see the nation of Israel as the fulfillment of biblical prophecy, the modern evidence of God's covenant faithfulness. The perception of modern-day Israel will determine the Church's strategic vision of end-time revival. This view of Israel will depend on whether or not the Church receives revelation and understanding of the times in which we live according to God's point of view.

Prophetic Alignment

The principle of prophetic alignment is foundational to an understanding of God's Word as a living reality. Many things are labeled *prophecy*, but only some of them are what I refer to as "prophecy with a capital P." Prophecy with a capital P is when God's inspired Word in Scripture converges with His actions in history. These major events of prophetic fulfillment reveal God's will in our times. They are the great redemptive events of our day, and they form the basis for other types of prophetic utterances and actions among God's people.

When God acts in history to fulfill His inspired Word in Scripture, we need revelation to recognize it. Many times God moves in important ways, and we miss it because we fail to see the prophetic significance of the event. It is essential to know what the Word of God says and to make the proper prophetic alignment between an important event and God's inspired Word.

The Bible records God's actions throughout the ages, but the greatest prophetic event of all time was the incarnation of Jesus, the Messiah. His birth, life, and ministry, including His death and resurrection, are a veritable *mountain* of fulfilled prophecy. In spite of the magnitude of this act of God in human history, many people living at the time of Jesus failed to recognize Him. Even when He preached to them and performed signs and wonders in their midst, the people of Israel as a whole missed the embodied purposes of God. However, those who believed in Him were able to see the prophetic significance of His life. By revelation, they became aligned prophetically with God's will in their day.

In the broadest sense, the New Testament Gospels were written in order for people to know what Jesus said and did, and to align the readers with His prophetic significance. Matthew uses the phrase or similar words, "that it might be fulfilled which was spoken by the Lord through the prophet," fourteen times throughout his gospel. In the first chapters of Matthew, he wrote:

> *And she will bring forth a Son, and you shall call His name JESUS, for He will save His people from their sins. So all this was done **that it might be fulfilled which was spoken by the Lord through the prophet**, saying: "Behold, the virgin shall be with child, and bear a Son, and they shall call His name Immanuel, which is translated, 'God with us'"* (Matthew 1:21-23).

> *When he arose, he took the young Child and His mother by night and departed for Egypt, and was there until the death of Herod, **that it might be fulfilled which was spoken by the Lord through the prophet**, saying, "Out of Egypt I called My Son"* (Matthew 2:14-15).

> *Then Herod, when he saw that he was deceived by the wise men, was exceedingly angry; and he sent forth and put to death all the male children who were in Bethlehem and in all its districts, from two years old and under, according to the time which he had determined from the wise men. **Then was fulfilled what was spoken by Jeremiah the prophet**, saying: "A voice was heard in Ramah, lamentation, weeping, and great mourning, Rachel weeping for her children, refusing to be comforted, because they are no more"* (Matthew 2:16-18).

Matthew, writing under the inspiration of the Holy Spirit, is presenting evidence of prophetic fulfillment in order to align the reader with God's purposes through revelation. This principle of prophetic alignment is crucial for the mind to apprehend and for the heart to accept. Jesus demonstrated the importance of this principle in His method of biblical interpretation.

Jesus' Sermon in Nazareth

Jesus taught and demonstrated that His life and ministry were completely in agreement with the prophecies given to Israel by the biblical prophets. There was nothing of more importance than Jesus' sayings and actions, yet many people failed to recognize who He was. A clear demonstration of Jesus' teaching method is found in Luke's account of Jesus' first sermon in His hometown synagogue:

> *And He came to Nazareth, where He had been brought up; and as was His custom, He entered the synagogue on the Sabbath, and stood up to read. And the book of the prophet Isaiah was handed to Him. And He opened the book and found the place where it was written,* "THE SPIRIT OF THE LORD IS UPON ME, BECAUSE HE ANOINTED ME TO PREACH THE GOSPEL TO

THE POOR. HE HAS SENT ME TO PROCLAIM RELEASE
TO THE CAPTIVES, AND RECOVERY OF SIGHT TO THE
BLIND, TO SET FREE THOSE WHO ARE DOWNTRODDEN,
TO PROCLAIM THE FAVORABLE YEAR OF THE LORD." *And
He closed the book, and gave it back to the attendant
and sat down; and the eyes of all in the synagogue were
fixed on Him. And He began to say to them, 'Today this
Scripture has been fulfilled in your hearing'"* (Luke
4:16-21, NASB).

Jesus was aware of the controversy He was creating
through His ministry in Galilee. Significant miracles were
taking place regularly, and large crowds were following Him
from place to place. He knew the great question in the minds
of His friends and neighbors related to His identity and the
source of His authority to preach, perform miracles, and
gather followers. In the synagogue, Jesus read the Scripture
portion that we know as the first verses from Isaiah, chapter
61 (of course, there were no chapter and verse divisions in
those days). The people in the synagogue understood that
this Scripture referred to the Messiah because of the words
in the first verse, "… He anointed me …" The Hebrew word
for Messiah comes from the same root word as the verb
"to anoint." Messiah simply means the "One anointed by
God."

Jesus applied this powerful Messianic prophecy to
himself. By preaching this way, Jesus related the events
surrounding His ministry to the inspired prophetic words of
the Scriptures. His listeners were free to accept or reject His
interpretation of prophecies that were written hundreds of
years before His time. Even though He was the perfect Son
of God, not everyone believed what He said. Some received
revelation and followed Him, but many only listened and
were unconvinced. Those who believed in Jesus discovered
God's will and began to follow a "new and living way."

Believers entered the Kingdom of God while skeptics missed out on the greatest event of their time. Many people in His day had access to Jesus and heard Him speak, but only some understood the life-changing truth His words could bring. The difference was revelation.

Peter's Sermon on Pentecost

Jesus taught His disciples to preach and teach by correlating God's actions in their day to Scriptural prophecy. Jesus' chief disciple, Peter, used this approach when he preached the gospel in Jerusalem on the Day of Pentecost. According to Acts, chapter 2, the disciples' prayer meeting in the upper room on Mount Zion was visited by the Holy Spirit and then overflowed onto the street. Jerusalem was filled with Jewish worshipers from all over the world. They were there in observance of God's command to come up to Jerusalem for the feast of Shavuot (Festival of Weeks or Pentecost).

The disciples were filled with the Spirit and were excitedly speaking the praises of God in a variety of languages they had never learned. The onlookers in the crowd that had formed were amazed, and some became aware that a miracle was taking place. Others said the believers were merely drunk. Confusion began to move through the people, and a spokesman was needed so that God's chosen moment would not be missed. Luke, the writer of Acts, recorded:

*But Peter, standing up with the eleven, raised his voice and said to them, "Men of Judea and all who dwell in Jerusalem, let this be known to you, and heed my words. For these are not drunk, as you suppose, since it is only the third hour of the day. **But this is what was spoken by the prophet Joel:** 'And it shall come to pass in the last days, says God, that I will pour out of My Spirit on all flesh; your sons and your daughters shall prophesy,* *your young men shall see visions, Your old men shall dream dreams'"* (Acts 2:14-17).

The people were perplexed by what they were witnessing, but they believed that God spoke to them through the prophets. As Peter related what was happening to the prophetic Scriptures before their eyes, he aligned the people prophetically. The events were thus established as a demonstration of God's will. Peter then preached the gospel to them and many were saved—by revelation that they were seeing a fulfillment of prophecy.

Ezekiel's Prophecy

The important phrase used by Peter was "… this is what was spoken by the prophet …" He used the same method of explanation that Jesus used in Nazareth. Events in Israel today need to be understood in the same manner. In the following pages, I have selected two prophecies in the Bible that speak directly about the regathering of the Jewish people and the re-establishment of the nation of Israel. The first is from the prophet Ezekiel:

> *Therefore say to the house of Israel, "Thus says the Lord GOD: '**I do not do this for your sake**, O house of Israel, but for My holy name's sake, which you have profaned among the nations wherever you went. And I will sanctify My great name, which has been profaned among the nations, which you have profaned in their midst; **and the nations shall know that I am the LORD**,' says the Lord GOD, 'when I am hallowed in you before their eyes'"* (Ezekiel 36:22-23).

In these verses, God says that He will do something with Israel so that all the nations will acknowledge Him. He emphatically states that it is not for Israel's sake that He will act. In other words, it is not because of divine favoritism or because of Israel's goodness, that God will do these things. God says it is not because Israel is so deserving or righteous, but for "My holy name's sake." God's action with Israel will be a demonstration of His sovereignty. God will do this thing because of who He is. What is it that God says He will do? The next verse reveals His plan, "*For I will take you from among the nations, gather you out of all countries, and bring you into your own land*" (Ezekiel 36:24).

Since the founding of the State of Israel, three million Jewish people have returned from every continent on the planet. Some might say that these words of Scripture are of historical relevance only, and that they relate to Israel's Babylonian captivity. However, Israel was dispersed to only one nation at that time. In these verses, God says He will gather them from "all the countries" and "from among the nations." The repeated use of the plural indicates a far wider dispersion and a greater regathering.

Why has God gone through such trouble to restore the Jewish people to the land of Israel today? Doesn't He know that bringing millions of Jews back to the Middle East will spark enduring conflict with the neighboring Muslim nations? Doesn't God understand that this conflict will threaten to destabilize the politics of the entire world? Ezekiel's prophecy tells us that God is not doing this for the sake of the Jewish people, but because of His own character and reputation. Furthermore, God is acting on behalf of the nations so that they will all recognize whom He is! According to Ezekiel, Israel is God's instrument again, His means to show His glory and His character to the entire world.

Seen in this light, we can understand why God has provoked such controversy by bringing the people of Israel back to their inherited land. It is His design to stir up the nations and cause people everywhere to examine their beliefs about the Jews, Israel, and ultimately, God himself. The existence of Israel is not a testimony to the strength, goodness, or virtuous qualities of her people. Israel's existence as a nation today is a testimony to God's faithfulness and His covenant-keeping character. It is God's name that was profaned during the centuries of the Jewish dispersion because God's enemies took the opportunity to scorn and persecute His chosen people. However, through the prophet Ezekiel, God says His endurance of that shame will have an end, and He will regather the people to whom He made so many everlasting promises. Ezekiel's prophecy does not end there. God says that He will do yet more for Israel after the regathering.

> *Then I will sprinkle clean water on you, and you shall be clean; I **will cleanse you** from all your filthiness and from all your idols. **I will give you a new heart** and put a new spirit within you; I will take the heart of stone out of your flesh and give you a heart of flesh. I **will put My Spirit within you** and cause you to walk in My statutes, and you will keep My judgments and do them. Then you shall dwell in the land that I gave to your fathers; you shall be My people, and **I will be your God*** (Ezekiel 36:25-28).

Through the prophet Ezekiel, God further says that after He regathers Israel, He will purify and transform the nation. According to this prophecy, God will not wait for Israel to be a holy people before bringing them back from the nations. After their return, He will cleanse the people and put a new heart and spirit within them. Today, many of the Jewish people that are returning to Israel are bitter and broken from their experiences in the nations during centuries of wandering and persecution. Some older Israelis still have Hitler's concentration camp tattoos visible on their arms. Deeper scars endure in the souls of the survivors. Others have come back still clinging to the idols of the nations where they sojourned for so many generations. In fulfillment of the Scriptures, God is cleansing and transforming hearts in Israel today. The re-emergence of Messianic Jews in Israel, the preaching of the Gospel in modern Hebrew, and the formation of indigenous, believing congregations are evidence of this prophetic fulfillment.

Jeremiah's Prophecy

Ezekiel's prophecy was intended for Israel, but the following verses in Jeremiah are specifically a word for the nations. The Hebrew word *goyim* is translated both "nations" and "Gentiles."

> *For thus says the LORD, "Sing aloud with gladness for Jacob, and* **shout among the chief of the nations;** *proclaim, give praise and say, 'O LORD, save your people, the remnant of Israel!'"* (Jeremiah 31:7).

The Lord says that we should praise Him for Israel among Gentile leaders and ask Him to bring salvation to the Jewish people. Because these words were written thousands of years ago, there is a timing factor at work here. When especially should the salvation of Israel be shouted about among the nations? The next verses in Jeremiah say:

> **Behold, I am bringing them from the north country, and I will gather them from the remote parts of the earth,** *among them the blind and the lame, the woman with child and she who is in labor with child, together;* **a great company, they will return here.** *With weeping they shall come, and by supplication I will lead them; I will make them walk by streams of waters, on a straight path in which they will not stumble; for* **I am a father to Israel, and Ephraim is My first-born.** *Hear the word of the LORD, O nations, and declare in the coastlands afar off, and say,* **"He who scattered Israel will gather him**

and keep him as a shepherd keeps his flock" (Jeremiah 31:8-10, NASB).

If you travel directly north on the compass from Jerusalem, you will eventually pass through Lebanon and Turkey. Then you will cross the Black Sea and enter the Ukraine. Hundreds of thousands of immigrants have come in recent years from the Ukraine. Traveling further north you will reach Russia. The city of Moscow is almost directly north of Jerusalem. The former Soviet Union is literally the "north country" in relation to Israel. In the last twenty years, over one million Russian-speaking immigrants have come to Israel. Jeremiah spoke for God when he wrote, "a great company, they will return here." This massive migration is the fulfillment of biblical prophecy. We are witnessing today what God foretold through His prophet.

Over one million new immigrants from the former Soviet Union represent one fifth of the total Jewish population and even more are expected. There are at least three million Jews still living in the "north country." The prophet Jeremiah prophesied that one day the return of Jewish exiles from the north and from all the nations will overshadow the migration of Israel out of Egypt at the time of the Exodus.

> *"Therefore behold, the days are coming," says the LORD, "that it shall no more be said, 'The LORD lives who brought up the children of Israel from the land of Egypt,' but, 'The LORD lives who brought up the children of Israel from the land of the north and from all the lands where He had driven them.' For I will bring them back into their land which I gave to their fathers"* (Jeremiah 16:14-15).

God Is a Father to Israel

In Ezekiel's prophecy, God states that His reason for this massive regathering of Israel is to reveal His own character and identity. In this case, it is God's fatherhood, His faithfulness, His loving responsibility, and covenant-keeping nature that are on display. In God's family, there are many, many children. Through faith in Jesus we have all received the "spirit of adoption" by which we cry out, "Abba, Father" (See Romans 8:15.) It does not matter from which nation or ethnic group we come. All are welcome, and there is no favoritism. However, God says through the prophet Jeremiah, "for I am a father to Israel, and Ephraim is My first-born." In any family, there can only be one first-born child. In God's family of many nations, Israel is His first-born.

I grew up in a family in which I was the second child. I learned many things by watching my parents' interaction with my older sister. Although there was the usual amount of sibling rivalry, I learned to be thankful that she, as the older one, received a stricter upbringing than I did. Israel was chosen first by God and given a covenant with Him to be an example for all the other nations. This is not divine favoritism, but rather a functional and sovereign choice of our Father in Heaven. We need to learn from Israel's obedience and blessings as well as Israel's disobedience and chastisement. Our older brother Israel has been estranged from the family of faith for nearly two thousand years. Will we Gentile believers welcome Israel back with honor and joy when we see the Father reaching out to him? Or, will we be like the brother of the prodigal son who resented the Father's seemingly unmerited love for the lost but returning one?

He Who Scattered Israel Will Gather

In the above Scripture from Jeremiah, God proclaims His responsibility for scattering Israel. The long, difficult years of wandering as a scorned minority group among the other nations can be attributed to the Father's sovereignty. As difficult as it is to comprehend, the persecutions, the expulsions, the pogroms, even the Holocaust did not take place apart from the Father's sovereign love. The Apostle Paul referred to hardships such as these as *the kindness and severity of God"* (Romans 11:22, NASB). This is a powerful lesson for all of us. God says that once He has regathered Israel, He will watch over him like a shepherd. (See Jeremiah 31:10.) In view of the harsh and unpredictable political conditions in Israel today, these words give us much comfort and security. These are turbulent and dangerous times. However, in every generation, the vision of God's people is challenged to grow. Jesus said that new wine requires new wineskins. Old paradigms must be discarded, and adjustment to new ones made. According to the prophet Daniel, not everything is made clear by God at once. Some truths are closed until their appointed time. For centuries, these prophecies about Israel have been hidden from all but a few men of faith and vision. Through revelation, these men saw the re-establishment of Israel and the calling of Israelis to faith in their Messiah. On June 16, 1864, Charles H. Spurgeon preached in London's Metropolitan Tabernacle using Ezekiel, chapter 37 as his text. He said:

> First, there is to be a political restoration of the Jews. Israel is now blotted out from the map of nations; her sons are scattered far and wide; her daughters mourn beside all the rivers of the earth. Her sacred song is hushed; no king reigns in Jerusalem; she bringeth forth no governors among her tribes. But she is to be restored; she is to be restored "as from the dead."

Although Israel's resurrection as a modern nation was revealed to some through their faith in God's Word, the unveiling of this restoration has been what the Apostle Paul called a "mystery"—one of God's secrets—until our day.

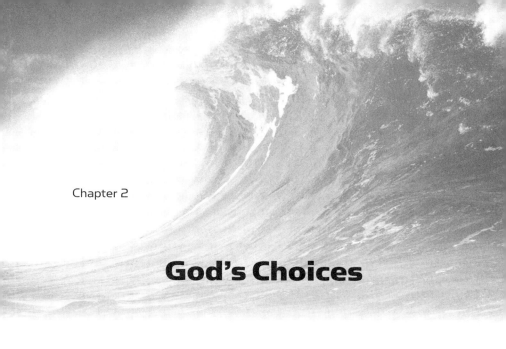

Chapter 2

God's Choices

THE MOST IMPORTANT FACT about the Kingdom of God is that there is a King. There can be no kingdom without the King. Being a servant of God in His kingdom requires an understanding and an acceptance of God's rule, His sovereignty. Our God is not a disinterested, distant *cosmic force* somewhere out there in the universe. He is a loving Father, a responsible leader who gets involved. He is *up close and personal* with the ones He loves. He can be confrontational, and He makes important, difficult decisions. To follow Him as one of His disciples means learning to hear His voice and submitting to His decisions. It means trusting Him and perfecting our ability to obey.

The ancient patriarch Job wrestled with God's decisions in his life. He could not accept what appeared to be injustice in God's dealings with him. The biblical account of Job's debate with his friends and with God lasts for nearly forty chapters. Finally, Job's sufferings led him to a powerful revelation of God's complete sovereignty. In the end, Job proclaims to God, *"I know that You can do everything, and that no purpose of Yours can be withheld from You"* (Job 42:2). This revelation became a key to Job's restoration and his place of biblical honor throughout the centuries.

God's purposes for His universe are righteous and eternal. He accomplishes them on Earth through humans that are chosen and guided by Him. In the days of Samuel the prophet, King Saul was rejected, and David, the son of Jesse, was chosen. Some people in Israel did not like that choice. In fact, a civil war was fought over it, but it was God's will that the crown go to David. Discerning God's will and agreeing to obey it is important for everyone. Those who fought against David for purely political reasons found themselves fighting against the Lord. Having respect for God's choices means choosing to be on God's side. When God chose to send His Son into the world as His means of salvation, those who accepted Him were saved, and those who rejected Him lost everything. Having a relationship with God means learning to love what He loves and learning to choose what He chooses.

God's Choice of Israel

The Bible makes it clear that God has chosen Israel for His own sovereign purposes. He made a covenant of love with Israel.

> *For you are a holy people to the LORD your God;* **the LORD your God has chosen you to be a people for Himself**, *a special treasure above all the peoples on the face of the earth. The LORD did not set His love on you nor choose you because you were more in number than any other people, for you were the least of all peoples; but because the LORD loves you* ... (Deuteronomy 7:6-8).

Throughout history, God has honored His choice of Israel, and He has been completely faithful to the covenant He made. It is a priority with God that every other nation should respect His choices and learn from Israel's example. The following two portions of Scripture show how Gentiles are blessed through recognition of God's choice of Israel. The first passage is recorded in the Book of Kings during the days of the prophet Elisha.

> *Now Naaman, commander of the army of the king of Syria, was a great and honorable man in the eyes of his master, because by him the LORD had given victory to Syria. He was also a mighty man of valor, but a leper. And the Syrians had gone out on raids, and had brought back captive a young girl from the land of Israel. She waited on Naaman's wife. Then she said to her mistress, "**If only my master were with the prophet who is in Samaria!** For he would heal him of his leprosy"* (2 Kings 5:1-3).

In those days, Syria was the dominant military and political power of the region. Naaman was the general who was instrumental in bringing his country to prominence. God chose him because of his greatness as a general, but also for much more. Along with being a great general, Naaman had an incurable disease. He was a leper. His Israeli servant girl loved her master and wanted to see him whole. She told him of a prophet in Israel with the power to heal. So Naaman was sent by his king to Israel to seek healing. Eventually, he arrived at the house of the prophet.

> *Then Naaman went with his horses and chariot, and he stood at the door of Elisha's house. And Elisha sent a messenger to him, saying, "Go and wash in the Jordan seven times, and your flesh shall be restored to you, and you shall be clean." **But Naaman became furious**, and went away and said, "'Indeed,' I said to myself, 'He will surely come out to me, and stand and*

call on the name of the LORD his God, and wave his hand over the place, and heal the leprosy.' **Are not the Abanah and the Pharpar, the rivers of Damascus, better than all the waters of Israel?** *Could I not wash in them and be clean?" So he turned and went away in a rage* (2 Kings 5:9-12).

When Naaman came to Elisha, the prophet sent a servant telling him to do what seemed like a repulsive thing. Naaman was enraged. He had not come to Israel with real humility and faith. His pride was hurt, and he was probably afraid that he would not be healed and would be returning home as a leper. Also, the Jordan River is unimpressive in appearance and is not such a mighty river. It is not wide like the Mississippi, blue like the Danube is said to be, or powerful like the Yangtse. The Jordan meanders slowly from Galilee to the Dead Sea, and during years of drought, it is little more than a muddy creek in some places. Naaman scorned the idea of dipping in the lowly Jordan when he had finer rivers back home.

However, Naaman's servants were humble and wise. They entreated him to follow the prophet's directions. Perhaps a measure of Naaman's greatness as a man chosen by God was that he surrounded himself with dedicated and loyal servants, and he listened to them.

And his servants came near and spoke to him, and said, "My father, if the prophet had told you to do something great, would you not have done it? How much more then, when he says to you, 'Wash, and be clean'?" **So he went down and dipped seven times in the Jordan, according to the saying of the man of God; and his flesh was restored like the flesh of a little child, and he was clean** (2 Kings 5:13-14).

It took humility to undress and dip in the Jordan River. In fact, the word Jordan is from the Hebrew root word that means "to go down." Naaman was not allowed to dip only once. The prophetic instructions were to be dunked an emphatic seven times. Upon coming up for the seventh time, Naaman was miraculously healed. All the wealth, wisdom, and power of Syria were unable to accomplish what God did in an instant. Naaman was happy and amazed, but he was wise enough to understand that God was speaking to him through his circumstances. The real point of this story is the conclusion that this great Syrian general reached after his healing in the Jordan River.

> *And he returned to the man of God, he and all his aides, and came and stood before him; and he said,* **"Indeed, now I know that there is no God in all the earth, except in Israel ..."** *(2 Kings 5:15).*

Naaman realized that it was not just a minor local god who had healed him. He knew it had to be the God of all the Earth. He furthermore realized that it was God's choice to heal him in a particular place. When he came to Israel and dipped in the Jordan, he humbled himself to accept God's sovereign choice of the Jewish nation. His humility and obedience brought about his healing. The miracle of his healing in turn brought him revelation of God and God's particular choices. Some might say that Naaman's example of healing is typical of God's ways in Old Testament times. Did God change His methods when His Son, Jesus, walked on Earth? Let's look at a biblical event from the ministry of Jesus.

> *Then Jesus went out from there and departed to the region of Tyre and Sidon. And behold, a woman of Canaan came from that region and cried out to Him, saying,* **"Have mercy on me, O Lord, Son of David!**

My daughter is severely demon-possessed." But He answered her not a word. And His disciples came and urged Him, saying, "Send her away, for she cries out after us" (Matthew 15:21-23).

Jesus took His disciples north of Israel to what is now Lebanon and a woman from that region came out to Him begging loudly for Him to heal her daughter. She was obviously not a Jew, but she knew who Jesus was. She called Him "Lord" and "Son of David," acknowledging Him as a Jewish master. At first, Jesus ignored her, but she persisted. Finally, His disciples asked Him to take action. I think Jesus deliberately ignored her until she had caught His disciples' attention. Jesus wanted to teach them all something through her example. Maybe Jesus was even looking out of the corner of His eye to see if His disciple, Matthew, was recording the events for us to read two thousand years later.

But He answered and said, "I was not sent except to the lost sheep of the house of Israel." Then she came and worshiped Him, saying, "Lord, help me!" (Matthew 15:24-25).

When everyone was listening, Jesus told the woman that she was not included in the group of people that God had given to Him as His primary focus. He had been sent to the people of Israel. The woman, however, humbled herself and began to entreat him. She asked for mercy, unmerited favor, and still Jesus did not relent. According to Matthew's record, Jesus then said something to her that caused me years of questioning and struggle. As a Gentile, I had a hard time believing that the Lord would actually say such a thing. I even wondered if Matthew had written it down correctly.

But He answered and said, "It is not good to take the children's bread and throw it to the little dogs" (Matthew 15:26).

This woman had approached Jesus with a legitimate request. He was known to have healed many, both Jews and Gentiles. She was not asking selfishly for herself, but for her daughter. She endured Jesus' initial cold shoulder and humbled herself, begging for His favor. Then He gave her an answer that sounded more like an insult than anything else. What was happening?

Have you ever had a disagreement with someone close to you that began innocently enough, but soon escalated into a heated argument? As tempers flared, words were exchanged to inflict damage rather than to provide correction or make a logical point. Finally, the other person said something so cutting, so cruel that you were left breathless and stunned, and then the argument was over. You simply could not respond, but after an hour or two, the perfect answer popped into your mind. If only you had said that during the argument, the result might have been so different! Becoming critical of yourself, you wondered why you were caught without words at that crucial time.

If I had been the Canaanite woman, I think I would have been similarly shocked into silence after Jesus' remark. I would have simply looked for the nearest exit. However, this woman was chosen by God to answer the Lord, and Jesus knew it. It is written in the Book of Proverbs, *"The preparations of the heart belong to man, but the answer of the tongue is from the LORD"* (Proverbs 16:1).

This Canaanite woman had no time to prepare an answer for Jesus, but she was anointed by God to answer for herself, for the sake of her daughter, and ultimately for all of us. She knew that if Jesus was the Messiah, He could not be just the Messiah for the Jews. He had to be the Lord of all the Earth. If He was not King of kings and Lord of lords, then she knew she was wasting her time. Her purpose was to receive healing, but God's purpose in this encounter (as in Naaman's healing) was to provide revelation about His identity and character. The woman answered Jesus with great humility, and perhaps a touch of humor. The Lord responded to her faith with a miracle.

> *And she said, "Yes, Lord, yet even the little dogs eat the crumbs which fall from their master's table." Then Jesus answered and said to her, "**O woman, great is your faith!** Let it be to you as you desire." And her daughter was healed from that very hour* (Matthew 15:27-28).

Jesus' initial reluctance to give healing was not a show of racism or divine favoritism. It was rather a demonstration of the functional focus of His ministry. God makes choices. If we want to work with Him and have His blessings, we must accept His ways. If we truly love Him, we will love what He chooses to love. The principle is that respecting and accepting God's choice of someone else is the key to finding and living in God's choice for you. Naaman and the Canaanite woman, both non-Jews, received miraculous healings when they humbled themselves before God's sovereign choice of Israel. A test of true humility and wisdom is to honor God's choice of someone else. At times, a genuine anointing of supernatural grace is needed to love whatever He loves. However, when we choose to humble ourselves and persist in seeking God's will, the Lord calls that "great faith," and He rewards it.

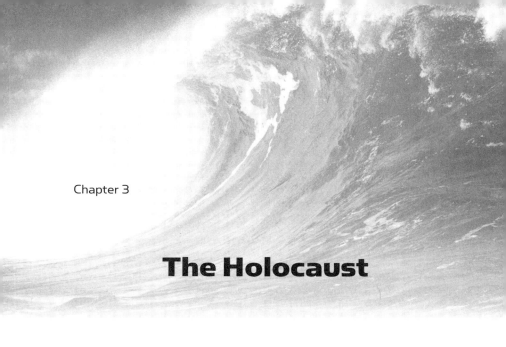

Chapter 3

The Holocaust

WE CANNOT UNDERSTAND God's mercy toward Israel today without looking at the extent to which the Jews have suffered as God's chosen people. The Holocaust, in which six million Jews were systematically murdered, is an event unprecedented in the history of the world. The Holocaust is unique in comparison to other genocides in history because there were no compelling economic, military, or political reasons for the Nazis to kill Jews. They were chosen for extermination purely because of their identity. They were Jews; God's chosen people.

The preservation of Israel as God's people is an important testimony to God's covenant faithfulness. Many times in history, Israel's enemies have risen up to destroy the Jewish people. It seems that whenever God is about to do something significant with His people, disaster threatens them. The most recent example is the Holocaust perpetrated by Nazi Germany. When the time was approaching for the Jewish homeland to be reborn, an evil power arose in Europe that nearly succeeded in annihilating the entire Jewish population. The majority of Jews in Europe were killed, but Hitler was unable to stop the creation of the State of Israel. In fact, the Holocaust may have done more than any single historic event to create worldwide sympathy for the Jews of the Diaspora (dispersion among the nations) so that the modern State of Israel could be born.

Since moving to Israel, my wife and I have had many occasions to share our faith with Jewish people. We owe so much to God for the mercy we have received. It is always a privilege and a thrill to have the chance to speak about Jesus, the Jewish Messiah, with His own people. Often, non-religious Jews will be interested in hearing what God has done in our lives, but when we speak of God's redemptive love, there is an obstacle. "What about the Holocaust?" they ask. "Where was this God of yours then?" Some Jews recognize that the God who has blessed our lives is, in fact, their God—the God of Moses, the God of Israel. These same people often say, "How could God have abandoned us to such cruelty? My parents were religious people, good Jews, but they were murdered by the Nazis. I will never believe in God again!" Questions regarding the attitude and actions of God during the Holocaust have a right to be asked.

In our city of Haifa, we still meet older people who have survived the death camps. A woman in our home fellowship group worked every day in a home for elderly Dutch survivors of the Holocaust. Another woman who attended the same group spent five years as a child in Auschwitz. Israeli children are taught to "never forget." The national Holocaust museum in Jerusalem is called *Yad Vashem* from the words "a place (or memorial) and a name" in Isaiah 56:5.

> *To the eunuchs who keep My Sabbaths, and choose what pleases Me, and hold fast My covenant, even to them I will give in My house and within My walls **a place and a name** better than that of sons and daughters; I will give them an everlasting name that shall not be cut off* (Isaiah 56:4-5).

These words were prophesied over eunuchs whose posterity had been cut off, similar to those who fell in the Nazi death camps. *Yad Vashem* is a powerful and moving memorial with spiritual significance for Jews and Gentiles alike. Many times, I have visited there struggling to comprehend the meaning of such vast suffering. I have wept at the sight of beautifully planted trees dedicated to the "righteous among the nations." These are the Gentiles who risked their lives to help Jews during the Holocaust. Corrie Ten Boom, the Dutch Christian who lost her family in the Nazi death camps for sheltering Jews, has a tree there. There is one for Raoul Wallenberg, the courageous Swedish diplomat who saved tens of thousands of Jews, and then is believed to have died in a Soviet prison. There is a tree for Oscar Schindler whose story has been told to the world in Steven Spielberg's *Schindler's List*. There is a tree for Japanese diplomat, Chiune Sugihara, who sacrificed his career by writing thousands of visas for Jews against official orders. His visas saved more than five thousand lives. I wonder if I would have laid down my life or lost my livelihood out of love for God and the Jewish people as others did in those desperate times.

Where was God during the Holocaust when six million Jews (including one-and-a-half million children) were cruelly rounded up and systematically murdered? As a believer in the sovereign Lord of history and eternity, it is not acceptable for me to say, "I don't know," or to blame it completely on Satan. The God of the Bible is omnipotent. Nothing is impossible for Him. He declared His faithfulness and unending love for Israel. He gave them promises of protection from their enemies and from Satan himself. God spoke to Israel through the prophet Isaiah.

*"Behold, I have created the blacksmith who blows the coals in the fire, who brings forth an instrument for his work; **and I have created the spoiler to destroy. No weapon formed against you shall prosper,** and every tongue which rises against you in judgment you shall*

condemn. This is the heritage of the servants of the LORD, and their righteousness is from Me," says the LORD (Isaiah 54:16-17).

The Psalmist declared God's watchfulness over Israel at all times, *"He will not allow your foot to be moved; He who keeps you will not slumber. Behold, **He who keeps Israel shall neither slumber nor sleep"*** (Psalm 121:3-4).

Israel was intended to be God's "special people," a "treasured possession" holding a place of honor among the nations. In the law given to Moses, the Torah, the prophet says:

> *Also today the LORD has proclaimed you to be His special people, just as He has promised you, that you should keep all His commandments, and that **He will set you high above all nations which He has made, in praise, in name, and in honor, and that you may be a holy people to the LORD your God**, just as He has spoken* (Deuteronomy 26:18-19).

How can we understand the devastation of the Holocaust in light of God's mercy and promises to Israel? The Apostle James wrote, *"Mercy triumphs over judgment"* (See James 2:13.) Mercy, however, does not *replace* judgment or God's justice toward all the nations. To be chosen by God and bound to Him by covenant as a national expression of His will means that in mercy or judgment, reward or chastisement, blessings or curses, God's righteousness will be made evident. In His actions toward His beloved Israel, God has created a standard by which His purposes for all nations may be measured.

God's covenant is an unbreakable relationship between Him and His people. In this covenant, both Israel and God had responsibilities that they were bound to perform. There were also sanctions or punishments if the covenant was not kept.

There are curses as well as blessings in the covenant that God gave to Israel through the great prophet Moses. All the people of Israel agreed to the covenant.

> *"Now therefore, **if you will indeed obey My voice and keep My covenant, then you shall be a special treasure to Me above all people; for all the earth is Mine.** And you shall be to Me a kingdom of priests and a holy nation. These are the words which you shall speak to the children of Israel."* *So Moses came and called for the elders of the people, and laid before them all these words which the LORD commanded him.* ***Then all the people answered together and said, "All that the LORD has spoken we will do."*** *So Moses brought back the words of the people to the LORD* (Exodus 19:5-8).

In the sacred books of the Torah and the prophets, there are powerful and clear passages that detail God's actions toward Israel if the people of Israel failed to keep their covenant with Him.

> ***The LORD will cause you to be defeated before your enemies;*** *you shall go out one way against them and flee seven ways before them; and you shall become troublesome to all the kingdoms of the earth.* ***Your carcasses shall be food for all the birds of the air and the beasts of the earth, and no one shall frighten them away*** (Deuteronomy 28:25-26).

> ***Your sons and your daughters shall be given to another people,*** *and your eyes shall look and fail with longing for them all day long; and there shall be no strength in your hand* (Deuteronomy 28:32).

*For death has come up through our windows; it has entered our palaces to cut off the children from the streets, the young men from the town squares. Speak, "Thus declares the LORD, 'The **corpses of men will fall like dung on the open field, and like the sheaf after the reaper, but no one will gather them**'"* (Jeremiah 9:21-22, NASB).

As painful as it is, we must begin to understand the Holocaust in terms of Israel's failure to keep the covenant of Moses. We understand that it is humanly impossible to keep the letter and the spirit of the Torah. The law was given to bring the people of Israel to the point of recognizing their shortcomings and sin so that they would cry out to God, trusting in His mercy. In His day, Jesus' greatest enemies were the religious people who thought they were righteous by keeping the Torah, the Law of Moses. Even today, ultra-religious Jews are convinced that with the help of rabbinic wisdom, they are able to obey the law and thus earn God's righteousness. Jesus warned in His Sermon on the Mount that He had not come to abolish the Torah, but to fulfill it. This is a promise of redemption as well as a stern word of warning. Jesus said not even the punctuation marks would be overlooked! All the blessings as well as all the curses would be fulfilled.

This view of the Holocaust as a fulfillment of God's covenantal curses is not limited to me alone. Rabbi Yisrael Meir Lau was born in Poland in 1937. He lost both his parents in the Holocaust, but, with his brother, he survived the Buchenwald concentration camp and immigrated to Israel in 1946. Following a long line of rabbis in his family, he was ordained in 1971, and eventually became the Ashkenazi Chief Rabbi of Israel in 1993. He was awarded the Israel Prize in May 2005, and the media has reported that he was even considered as a candidate for the position of president of the state of Israel. Rabbi Lau told the *Jerusalem Post*, "The curses mentioned in Leviticus and Deuteronomy came true during the Holocaust" (*Jerusalem Post*, January 6, 2005, page 1).

Jesus was clear about the fulfillment of all of Israel's law. In His sermon on the mount He said,

> *Do not think that I came to destroy the Law or the Prophets. I did not come to destroy but to fulfill. For assuredly, I say to you, till heaven and earth pass away,* **one jot or one tittle will by no means pass from the law till all is fulfilled** (Matthew 5:17-18).

What was God doing during the Holocaust? He was weeping in pain for His covenant people. Weeping like King David wept for his son, Absalom. In 2 Samuel 18:33, it is recorded that even though his son had rebelled, the king went to his room and wept, saying, *"O my son Absalom —my son, my son Absalom—if only I had died in your place! O Absalom my son, my son!"* This is the heart of God who is a Father to Israel. This is the heart of God who takes loving responsibility for everything under His sovereign care. Were the Nazis used as God's instrument of judgment on Israel? Let us remember that Satan himself is a creation of God, acting deliberately and consistently against God's goodness. Many times in Scripture, it is recorded that God used the enemies of Israel to bring about His will in order to chastise the nation. In the song that Moses sang in the desert, it is clear that no defeat could come upon Israel unless it was allowed by Almighty God. Inspired by the Holy Spirit, Moses sang:

> *How could one chase a thousand, and two put ten thousand to flight,* **unless their Rock had sold them, and the LORD had surrendered them?** (Deuteronomy 32:30).

God is holy, and His ways are above the ways of men. When other people are allowed to attack Israel as part of God's chosen chastisement, God does not absolve the persecutors of their guilt. God is just and keeps His Word. The Word of God says, "Do not judge, lest you be judged!" The Apostle Paul taught that the Torah was given by God to Israel as a "schoolmaster" until Messianic faith could be formed in their hearts. Paul understood that by putting their trust in Jesus, Israel would be saved from the curses contained in the Torah.

> *Christ has redeemed us from the curse of the law,* having become a curse for us (for it is written, "Cursed is everyone who hangs on a tree") (Galatians 3:13).

Paul does not mean that the Torah is a curse. He wrote elsewhere that the Law is good and righteous. The grammatical form of the Greek language used in this Scripture is called the genitive case, signifying possession. The phrase in bold type could better be translated "the curse that belongs to the law." An example of this grammatical form is used when we say "the United States of America." Actually, we mean "the United States in America," because there are other nations on the American continent. In parallel, we can understand Paul to be writing about the "curses in the law" to the Galatians.

As a believer in Jesus, I cannot ignore the warnings of judgment that He gave to Israel before His crucifixion and the descriptions of God's curses upon disobedience found in the Torah and the prophets. When I look at photographs of the Holocaust, I often think of these Scriptures and shudder. We Gentile believers want all the blessings of Abraham, but we don't like to read about God's curses. Even if we don't believe that we have replaced Israel in God's redemptive plan, we may be quick to say that we are joined to our *Jewish roots*. Don't Christians realize the responsibility that comes along with being counted among God's chosen? Paul wrote to Gentile believers about the natural and foreign branches of the Abrahamic olive tree in Romans, chapter 11. He warned us with these words:

> *You will say then, "[Jewish] Branches were broken off that I might be grafted in." Well said. Because of unbelief they were broken off, and you stand by faith.* **Do not be haughty, but fear. For if God did not spare the natural branches, He may not spare you either.** *Therefore consider the goodness and severity of God: on those who fell, severity; but toward you, goodness, if you continue in His goodness. Otherwise you also will be cut off. And they also, if they do not continue in unbelief, will be grafted in, for God is able to graft them in again* (Romans 11:19-23).

What significance does this have for the nations of today? When we see the Holocaust in light of God's covenant faithfulness, the suffering of the Jewish people is not a sign of God's rejection, but actually the opposite. God has not broken the covenant He made with Israel through Moses. The people of Israel failed to keep the covenant, and they rejected God's offer of mercy in the sacrificial giving of His Son, Jesus. Painfully, God allowed the sanctions written into the covenant to be fulfilled. God's refusal to abolish the covenant and reject the Jewish people is a sign to all nations of His faithfulness. The Apostle Paul points out that God's integrity will cause Him to treat Gentile Christians with the same justice and mercy.

Nearly two thousand years after Paul wrote those inspired words, we can now understand more of God's severity toward the Jews. However, the re-establishment of the State of Israel demonstrates God's amazing mercy and grace toward the people that He originally chose. In addition, the modern emergence of Messianic Jews demonstrates that God is again grafting them into their own tree of faith. Ultimately, Israel's restoration and the Jews' acceptance of Jesus as Messiah is linked to revival in all nations. In Joel, chapter 2, the prophet wrote that Israel's shame and reproach among the nations will be removed, and after that, God will pour out His Spirit on all mankind. The restoration of Israel as a sovereign state in 1948 and her miraculous survival through a series of bitter regional wars are prophetically linked to the greatest release of God's Spirit in revival ever seen in human history. The Apostle Paul wrote:

> *For if their* [the Jews] *being cast away is the reconciling of the world, what will their acceptance be but life from the dead?* (Romans 11:15).

We have to acknowledge from the Scriptures that God foresaw the inability of Israel to keep the covenant just as He knew Adam and Eve would yield to temptation and fall into sin. Because of God's sovereignty and foreknowledge, the suffering of the Jewish people under the curses in the Law of Moses has the redemptive effect of teaching God's character to the nations of the world. Like Jesus, the Messiah of the Jewish people, Israel was chosen to suffer, to die as a nation, and to be resurrected in modern times. God foresaw that some of the Jews would accept Jesus and become His disciples. These were the first apostles to the nations and the writers of the New Testament. He also foresaw that the nation as a whole would reject Jesus and stumble over the "stone which the builders rejected." Israel was chosen for this role in God's sovereign plan for the nations.

One Jewish artist who intuitively grasped this deep truth is Marc Chagall. Perhaps the most famous Jewish modern artist, Chagall's work can be seen hanging in Israel's Knesset (Parliament) building. Reprints are available in numerous stores and galleries. Some of his best-known works are the stained glass windows of the twelve tribes of Israel, located in the Hadassah Hospital Chapel at Ein Kerem near Jerusalem. In 1938, Chagall painted a canvas he called *White Crucifixion*.

It is a picture of Jesus hanging on a Cross, wrapped in a Jewish prayer shawl, and surrounded by illustrations that depict the persecution of Jewish people. The persecution scenes are based on the long history of anti-Jewish expulsions and massacres, and they foreshadow the Holocaust, which was just a few years away when Chagall painted the picture. Jesus, at the center of the picture, is illuminated from above and embodies the suffering of His own people. The sufferings of the Jewish people find their focus in Jesus. I have always thought that this picture captures a powerful reality that is worth more than a thousand words. Chagall's painting eloquently shows the convergence of Israel and the Church at the Cross of Jesus. Most Christians seem to see only Jesus in the middle of the picture, and they miss the significance of His surroundings. Most Jews see only the scenes of Jewish suffering and miss the centrality of Jesus. Chagall, a great artist, saw them both together.

Was Chagall personally a believer in Jesus? I have never read anything that would indicate he was. However, I find it interesting that toward the end of his life he painted another crucifixion scene called *Exodus*. This picture, painted after the Holocaust between 1952 and 1966, is much darker in tone. It shows the Jewish people coming out of slavery and persecution as Moses leads them, carrying the tablets of the Torah. Hovering over them all is a huge, superhuman-sized Jesus, still on the Cross—but with arms outstretched as if in blessing or welcome. What theologians and religious leaders find difficult or impossible to see or communicate, Chagall the artist seems to do through an intuitive leap of imagination. His creativity as seen in these pictures functions powerfully, like a gift from God. The paintings portray Israel's Messiah in a manner similar to the way Isaiah foretold Jesus' sacrificial mission with these inspired and poetic words:

Surely He has borne our griefs and carried our sorrows; yet we esteemed Him stricken, smitten by

God, and afflicted. But He was wounded for our transgressions, He was bruised for our iniquities; the chastisement for our peace was upon Him, and by His stripes we are healed. All we like sheep have gone astray; we have turned, every one, to his own way; and the LORD has laid on Him the iniquity of us all (Isaiah 53:4-6).

Marc Chagall lived from 1887 until 1985, and his works can be easily viewed by searching for them by name on the Internet. The original canvas of his powerful *White Crucifixion* can be seen on display at the Art Institute of Chicago.

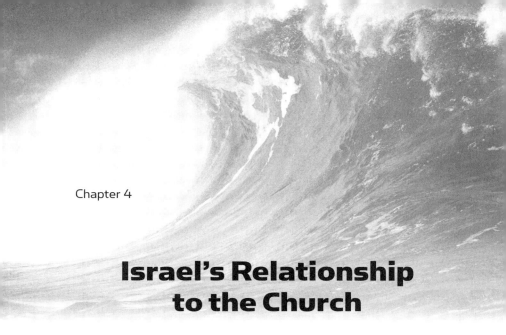

Chapter 4

Israel's Relationship to the Church

IN ORDER TO GAUGE THE IMPACT that revelation about the scriptural identity of modern Israel has on the Church, we have to understand what Christians believe about the Jewish people. Since the early centuries of the Church, the basic belief about Israel has been one of *replacement*. Simply stated, this means that God has replaced Israel with the Church in His redemptive plan. Because of the New Testament promises, God no longer honors His previous promises and the covenants He made with the Jewish people. Is God really finished with Israel? We should examine the New Testament to see what the Apostle Paul, inspired by the Holy Spirit, wrote on the subject.

The New Testament letter written by Paul to the Romans is one of the most powerful and beloved books in the Bible. Millions have been inspired by its words over the centuries. The great reformer, Martin Luther (1483-1546) drew important principles from its pages and later in 1738, John Wesley reported his heart was "strangely warmed" while he listened to a reading from Luther's preface to his commentary on Romans. This marked the beginning of Wesley's ministry that would transform England and launch the Methodist movement.

"Blink" Theology

The first half of Romans is written in such a systematic way that many have studied it by beginning with chapter 1 and proceeding chapter by chapter down what has become known as the "Roman Road." This is a convenient way to gain a clear understanding of salvation starting with the condition of man, the nature of sin, consequences of unbelief and leading to God's promise of eternal life through faith in Jesus. In Romans chapter 7, the Apostle Paul shares his own personal struggle with the great truths he is teaching, but in chapter 8 he triumphantly declares the power of God's Spirit to fulfill the requirements of Heaven in the lives of those who believe. Sadly, many students of this inspired letter develop what could be called a theological *blink* after finishing chapter 8. We seem to close our eyes only for a moment, but when they are open again we are now at the beginning of chapter 12 having skipped over chapters 9, 10 and 11.

Why do we blink and skip those three chapters? Because seemingly without reason in the midst of this theologically powerful and systematic letter, Paul begins to write about Israel as the nation of the Jewish people and then about the correct relationship between Jews and Gentiles in the New Testament Church. For centuries, great Christian scholars could not understand why Paul wrote about Israel and the Jews in this way and at this point in his letter. After all, for most of the last two thousand years Israel did not exist as a nation and there were hardly any Jews worshipping Jesus in the churches. Those Jews who did become followers of Jesus tended to give up their Jewish identity and live just like Gentile Christians.

The result was that Christians tended to either spiritualize or ignore Romans chapters 9 through 11. Spiritualizing Paul's writing meant that Gentile Christians were *spiritual* Israel or *spiritual* Jews. This would mean that wherever there was a reference to Israel or Jewish believers, Christians should simply appropriate those truths to themselves. Other scholars thought

Paul was only writing about something that had relevance to his particular time and so the intended theological impact could be ignored. In some Bible translations, there are even notes added by modern editors that indicate chapters 9, 10 and 11 are merely *parenthetical* chapters put in by Paul as an afterthought. Today, however, Israel is a nation of Jewish people once more. Moreover, there is a growing movement of Jews who not only believe in Jesus and the New Testament, but also maintain their identities as Jews. Recent studies have shown us that far from being parenthetical, those three chapters of Romans are *pivotal* and may even be the very reason that Paul wrote the letter to Rome in the first place.

We know that most of the time, Paul wrote his letters to correct problems that emerged in the early churches. For example, the Thessalonians had wrong ideas about the return of the Lord, the Galatians were confused by false teachers about the Law, and the Corinthians had moral problems that Paul specifically addressed. The problem in Rome was a conflict between Jewish and Gentile believers over their respective places in leadership. Perhaps this problem developed when the Jews who planted the church in Rome were expelled under the Emperor Claudius. Later, when they were able to return, the new Gentile leaders did not accept them back as equals since most of the congregation was by then Gentile and Israel as a nation had rejected Jesus as Messiah. Paul heard about this conflict and the growing division between Jewish and Gentile believers so he wrote to correct it.

If this is so, why then did he take so much time and effort in the first half of the letter to write a comprehensive and systematic explanation of his beliefs? The answer to this question may be very simple. Every other letter in the New Testament written by the Apostle Paul is addressed either to his own personal disciples or to a congregation he himself planted. The lone exception is his letter to the Romans. In Rome, they knew of Paul by reputation but they did not know him personally. He had never been to Rome and they were not his own *spiritual sons*. So, in order to establish his apostolic credentials and win their trust, Paul wrote down his gospel in a clear way to ensure that they would be ready to accept his solution to their problem by the time they got to the second half of his letter. Perhaps the Roman believers, like us, were enthusiastically nodding their heads in agreement by the time they reached the triumphant end of chapter 8.

Following his lengthy theological introduction, in Romans chapter 9, Paul explains about God's sovereign choices. Not only did God choose Israel for His own purposes but He also chose within Israel, a special group, a redeemed remnant of believing Jews. This is the meaning of Paul's statement, *"But it is not as though the word of God has failed. For they are not all Israel who are descended from Israel"* (Romans 9:6, NASB). In this verse, Paul is telling the Gentile leaders that God did not make a mistake in selecting Israel as the people from whom the Messiah would come. Furthermore, in this verse, Paul is not opening up the definition of Israel to include non-Jews. He is actually narrowing the focus to say that Jews who believe in Jesus are the true Israel or the "Israel of God." (See Galatians 6:16.) Paul is emphasizing the special importance and calling of the believing remnant—Jews who follow Jesus as Lord.

In chapter 10, Paul writes about the key role of faith in bringing together both Jews and Gentiles into one redeemed body. Then, in chapter 11, Paul begins to describe God's end-time plan for His Church, the Bride of Christ, consisting of believing Jews and Gentiles from every nation. In chapter 11, the apostle is prophesying modern events with laser-like accuracy: God's judgment on unbelieving Israel followed by His mercy and the ultimate modern emergence of Jews who are disciples of Jesus, their Jewish Messiah.

When we read the first verses of Romans chapter 11, we have to wonder how so much of the Christian Church today can believe that God has rejected Israel and replaced the Jewish people in His redemptive plan.

> *I say then, has God cast away His people? Certainly not! For I also am an Israelite, of the seed of Abraham, of the tribe of Benjamin. **God has not cast away His people whom He foreknew….*** (Romans 11:1-2a)

No one should have known better than Paul that the Jewish nation had rejected Jesus as its Messiah and Savior. Paul was a zealous and devout Jew and had been a persecutor of those who believed in Jesus. Then, after he came to faith, Paul himself was bitterly persecuted by his Jewish compatriots. By the time he wrote the letter to the Romans, numerous attempts had been made by zealous Jews to kill or imprison him. In spite of all this, he wrote that God had not rejected Israel. In fact, Paul goes on to explain God's purposes behind Israel's failure to recognize their Messiah. In his letter, he shows the Lord's ultimate objective—to preach the gospel to the entire world and to bring Jew and Gentile together in one body.

Other than the clear exhortation of the Apostle Paul, a good reason for the Church to reject the idea of God's rejection of the Jewish people is the issue of covenant. God chose Israel and made promises that are a part of the scriptural record. God's continued faithfulness to the Jewish people, in spite of their rejection of His Son Jesus, is evidence of His great covenant-keeping nature. God's Word will never pass away. He will keep every promise He has made even if it should take two years, twenty years, two hundred years, or two thousand years! Gentile Christians are also people that have a covenant with God. God has made promises to the Church that we believe He will keep. If we Christians do not believe that God keeps all His covenants, how can we know for certain that our covenant with Him in the body and blood of His Son, Jesus, will never be broken or invalidated?

I say then, have they [Israel] *stumbled that they should fall? Certainly not! But through their fall, to provoke them to jealousy, salvation has come to the Gentiles. Now **if their fall is riches for the world, and their failure riches for the Gentiles, how much more their fullness!*** (Romans 11:11-12).

Paul is clear about Jewish failure to recognize their Messiah. However, God's wisdom was capable of turning the chosen people's failure into a blessing for the rest of the world. Prophetically, Paul envisions the day when Israel will at last honor Jesus as Lord. He foresees the spiritual riches that Israel's acceptance of the Messiah will mean to the world. The Apostle Paul then explains that Israel's acceptance of the Lord will mean "life from the dead." The word for *life* found here is *zoe*, which is used by the Apostle John in the New Testament for the kind of life that God has within himself. *"For as the Father has life in himself, so He has granted the Son to have life in himself"* (John 5:26), and *"In Him was life, and the life was the light of men"* (John 1:4).

"*For if their being cast away is the reconciling of the world,* **what will their acceptance be but life from the dead?**" (Romans 11:15).

Earlier I wrote that today we are witnessing the greatest move of the Holy Spirit among Jews in Israel since the days of the Bible. Israelis are finding God's life through faith in Jesus, the Messiah. Their small numbers belie their biblical significance. We are at the beginning of Israel's "acceptance" as prophetically predicted by the Apostle Paul. The result of this acceptance, according to the Scripture, is "life from the dead." Jesus said, "... Man shall not live [*zoe*] by bread alone, but by every word that proceeds from the mouth of God" (Matthew 4:4). Revelation of God's Word brings life. This means the "resurrection" of modern Israel is to be accompanied by an outpouring of biblical revelation. Israel's acceptance is a *trigger* event for revelation and revival on an unprecedented scale throughout the world.

The Two Olive Trees

In this same chapter of Romans, the Apostle Paul further describes the relationship between Jew and Gentile in the Church. He uses the image of two olive trees—a wild olive tree (Gentiles) and a cultivated olive tree (Jews). Why are Jews considered the cultivated tree? This is because God has been working with them directly for thousands of years longer than with any other people. In these passages, Paul is addressing Gentiles in the Church as "you" and referring to the Jewish people as "they."

> And if some of the branches were broken off, **and you, being a wild olive tree, were grafted in among them,** and with them became a partaker of the root and fatness of the olive tree, do not boast against the branches. But if you do boast, reme**mber that you do not support the root, but the root supports you.** You will say then, "Branches were broken off that I might be grafted in." Well said. Because of unbelief they were broken off, and you stand by faith. **Do not be haughty, but fear.** For if God did not spare the natural branches, He may not spare you either (Romans 11:17-21).

Paul warned Gentile believers not to develop a haughty attitude toward the broken off Jewish branches because the Abrahamic tree of faith is Jewish in nature and origin. A mystery of faith that joins the originally chosen people with the other nations is being revealed here. Paul wrote to the Roman Church that the sign of genuine understanding of this mystery is the fear of the Lord. He wrote, "Do not be haughty, but fear." Why fear? Fear of God, the beginning of wisdom, is the correct response because it indicates our recognition of the price demanded of those who are chosen by God. Knowing the suffering that the divinely selected Jewish people have experienced since Paul penned this letter, students of history, and the Bible should be filled with the fear of God.

> *Therefore consider the goodness and severity of God: on those who fell, severity; but toward you, goodness, if you continue in His goodness. Otherwise you also will be cut off. And they also, if they do not continue in unbelief, will be grafted in, for God is able to graft them in again. For if you were cut out of the olive tree which is wild by nature, and were grafted contrary to nature into a cultivated olive tree,* **how much more will these, who are natural branches, be grafted into their own olive tree?** (Romans 11:22-24).

God, who is a Father to Israel, scattered His covenant people among the nations. He takes responsibility for all that occurred as a result of that dispersion. If God would bring such calamity upon His chosen ones, can we expect Him to be less severe toward the rest who are grafted in "contrary to nature?" Paul says no, and urges us, along with the Gentile believers in Rome of long ago, to stand fast in faith at all costs. When taught that the Jews are God's chosen people, some Christians react to that with what they fear is partiality or even racism. There are those who object to the teaching on God's choice of Israel because it does not present a *level playing field* for all nations before God. These fears and objections are based on assumptions that are far from the truth. Israel was chosen as an example—an object lesson from God to all other nations. Willingly or unwillingly, in obedience to God or in disobedience, Israel is a sacrificial, servant nation. Knowing Israel's history in the last twenty centuries and the painful current situation, is there any other nation or ethnic group in the world that would willingly trade places? All peoples are equal before the righteous requirements of God, but every nation has a unique place and a distinct role to play in God's purposes. Israel was chosen as His illustration of this truth.

> *For I do not desire, brethren, that you should be ignorant of this mystery, lest you should be wise in your own opinion, that* **blindness in part has happened to Israel until the fullness of the Gentiles has come in. And so all Israel will be saved.** *...* (Romans 11:25-26a).

Prophetically, Paul wrote that the days would come when God would turn again to the Jews and begin to graft them back into the tree of their fathers, restoring them by faith in Jesus. Today, I write as a pastor of a local Israeli congregation and as a witness of the Jewish regathering, which is taking place in our day. Messianic Jews are the natural branches that were broken off. However, they have been redeemed by faith in Jesus in order to be re-grafted into their fathers' inheritance. Paul wrote that we should expectantly look forward to national revival in Israel, but that this will come in concert with worldwide revival and the "fullness" of the Gentiles. God's ultimate purpose is to bring both His original covenant people and His new covenant (New Testament) people together as "one new man" (see Ephesians 2:15) through faith in Jesus, the Savior of the world.

Messianic Jews

There has always been a remnant of Jewish disciples of Jesus down through the ages since the days of the New Testament. Two major historical forces served to reduce the numbers and public profile of Jewish believers. The first is the rejection of Messianic faith by Rabbinic Judaism that became complete exclusion in the years after the time of Jesus. The second was the growing contempt for Jewishness primarily among Gentile believers, and consequently, a deliberate severing of the Church's Jewish roots. Christian anti-Semitism, although a complete contradiction in terms and a direct violation of New Testament Scripture (See Romans 11:17-24.) took hold in the early centuries of the Church. Thus, as Gentiles outnumbered Jewish believers, the Jews tended to assimilate into the forms of the Gentile Church over a period of generations.

However, in the 1960's, a new movement of Jewish people emerged who believed in the Messiah, *Yeshua* (the Hebrew name for Jesus which means "salvation"). Messianic Jews believe that the entire Bible is inspired, and they worship God as Father, Son, and Holy Spirit. There are many streams in this growing movement and some groups hold beliefs that some Christians would consider extreme. However, in general, Messianic Jews identify as an integral part of the Church that, nevertheless, has characteristics distinct from Gentile Christians. According to the Book of Acts, the disciples of Jesus were first called "Christians" only outside of Israel. It was at Antioch (in modern Turkey) that the early movement became numerically more Gentile than Jewish. Before this, the believers were almost all Jewish and were known by a variety of names. Today, the term "Messianic" is used by believing Jews because "Christian" is derived from the Greek word *Christos,* which means "Anointed One." The same word in biblical Hebrew is *Mashiach* from which comes the English word "Messiah." While numerically strongest in the United States and especially significant in the nation of Israel, the Messianic Jewish movement is international. It marks a return to the biblical origins of the New Testament community in Jerusalem, which was almost entirely Jewish. The challenge for today's Messianic Jewish movement is to define in modern terms what it means to be both Jewish and a believer in Jesus, the Messiah.

Messianic Jews are an essential, historic link between Israel and the Church. As a movement, they have a destiny to stand prophetically toward the Jewish people and the nation of Israel as well as toward the Christian churches throughout the world. The truth of Jew and Gentile bound together in the Messiah is deep and complex. Derek Prince, who lived many years in Jerusalem, wrote in his book, *Prophetic Destinies*:

> One of the most exciting features of the period in which we now live is that the destinies of Israel and the church are once again beginning to converge. Their convergence will produce the most dramatic and significant developments of all human history.

Reconciliation in Rome

In May 1997, I had the privilege of participating in a week of intercessory prayer and fasting at a retreat center located outside the city of Rome. The purpose of the week was to pray toward repentance in the traditional churches for their historic anti-Semitism, and for the restoration of the biblical relationship between Israel and the Gentile Church. The group consisted of thirty-one born again believers representing the Messianic Jewish body in Israel, and those whose backgrounds were from various European Protestant traditions, the Roman Catholic Church, and the Greek Catholic Church in Lebanon.

As we began our time together, we reviewed the historic relations between the Church and Israel. These are comprised of three main historical divisions:

1. In the second and third centuries, the teaching of Romans, chapter 11 was forgotten. This was evidenced by the absence of Jewish Bishops at the Council of Nicaea (325 A.D.). Theologically, this resulted in the spiritualization of the Old Testament Scriptures. Here is the root of *replacement* theology, which holds erroneously that God has rejected the Jewish people, and that there is no longer a distinct redemptive plan for them as a people.

2. The fourth through the tenth centuries marked the ascendancy of replacement theology and the Church's official teaching of contempt for any Jewish tradition. This resulted in the institutionalization of anti-Semitism in the Church.

3. From the eleventh century onwards, beginning with the Crusades, there were more frequent and violent anti-Jewish measures taken by the Church. These included persecution, propagation of anti-Jewish myths, the Inquisition, and expulsion of all the Jews from Spain in 1492. This culminated in a European cultural environment that was ripe for Nazi exploitation and the Holocaust.

In modern Israel, the lingering wounds from this historic betrayal and persecution contribute to rejection of the gospel. In the hearts of most Israelis, Christian symbols like the cross generate a feeling of distaste and mistrust. In Israeli elementary school textbooks, the sign for addition is not a cross as in most other nations. It is an inverted T-shaped symbol, which offers a glimpse into the depth of this aversion. (For more information on Gentile and Christian anti-Semitism, I recommend Dr. Michael Brown's book, *Our Hands are Stained with Blood* published by Destiny Image).

We examined how the spiritually evil fruit of Christian anti-Semitism has been a feature of the Church in Europe since its earliest days. The Holocaust, a genocide of proportions beyond human comprehension, could take place with little protest because the ground had been prepared by centuries of discrimination directed toward Jews by most of the traditional Church (Catholic and Protestant). The guilt that the traditional Christian community in Europe carries is very heavy and is like a spiritual poison in the bowels of the Church, causing stiffness and sickness and holding back revival.

Our group in Rome attempted to grapple with the reality of this history. We entered into deep times of worship and confession together, but hit a wall when those from a Catholic background were unable to confess the sins of that particular church against the Jewish people. They acknowledged the gross sin of Christian anti-Semitism but found it difficult to admit the responsibility of the Catholic Church itself. One of the Messianic Jewish leaders challenged these brothers and sisters to recognize their guilt. He shared that a curse lies upon any group or individual that embraces anti-Semitism, and that it can only be removed through true repentance. God said to Abraham, *"And I will bless those who bless you, and the one who curses you I will curse...."* (Genesis 12:3, NASB). They then withdrew to a separate meeting place while the rest of us prayed for a breakthrough.

After many hours of prayer, we all came together again, and clearly God had broken through. Spiritual barriers had been removed from their hearts. Where there had been resistance, there was flexibility. Where there had been fear and hesitation, there were tears of joy. These brothers and sisters confessed their collective sin of historic anti-Semitism and asked forgiveness of the Messianic Jewish believers, who embraced them in fellowship. The rest of the evening was an unrestrained celebration of joy in the Spirit of God.

The next day, we all awoke in a new spirit of unity, and then proceeded on a prayer tour by bus. We visited the catacombs of Domitilla where believers were buried in ancient times, and then we arrived at the Arch of Titus near the ancient Roman forum. On the arch is a sculpted relief of Jewish prisoners being paraded through the streets of Rome after the fall of Jerusalem in 70 A.D. On their shoulders is depicted the seven-branched, golden candlestick (*menorah*) that was taken as the spoils of war from the holy place of the Temple in Jerusalem. This *menorah* is the symbol of God's presence and the fullness of His Spirit. It symbolized the light of God's truth—the light that God intended Israel to give to all the nations. (See Isaiah 49:6.)

We stood before the arch and proclaimed God's faithfulness in bringing the Jewish people back to the land of promise. Together, the Messianic Jewish remnant and the "grafted in" Gentiles petitioned God to restore His light to Jerusalem. We proclaimed that God's presence and His light would return to Israel from its dispersion in the nations.

We visited the ancient coliseum, which was built by Jewish slaves brought back to Rome after the fall of Jerusalem. We also saw the cathedrals of both Peter and Paul—the first Jewish believers commissioned to bring the light of God's truth to the Gentile world. In each place, we gathered for prayer and intercession for the traditional churches, for Israel, and the believing Jewish remnant. We prayed that Jesus and His apostles, stripped of their "Jewishness" in Rome, would be restored to their original and biblical identities. We prayed that Mary, who has been an idolatrous symbol to many throughout the world, would be restored to her Messianic Jewish identity as Miriam, a godly example of a woman of deep faith, genuinely submitted to God.

Arch of Titus

During this week of prayer and fasting, we gained a deeper understanding of the ministry of intercession for Israel and the Church. Powerful seeds of reconciliation and restoration were sown. It is exciting to consider the Lord's plans for the future. We are at a turning point in history. Certainly, the fullness of time has come for the Lord to turn His favor toward Zion and to rebuild His testimony in the land of Israel. We are a part of the "summing up of all things in Christ" (see Ephesians 1:10, NASB) in preparation for the return of the Lamb.

Many recognize that Christianity in Europe is in steep decline. In a significant sense, the proclamation of Israel and the remnant of believing Jews are a key to recovery and revival in the European Church. I cannot help but compare the Christian movement elsewhere with the situation of my European Christian friends who must grapple with these deep issues of collective guilt and repentance. God gave Europe the gospel for almost twenty centuries. It is amazing to consider the great achievements that have come from *Christian* Europe. However, the weight of history appears to be crippling the traditional Church in Europe today whereas in Asia, South America, and Africa, the growth of Evangelical and Pentecostal churches is fast reaching gigantic proportions. I can only surmise that the "Lord of the Harvest" will do a massive and accelerated work (as compared to Europe) in all of Asia, Africa, and South America. It is imperative, however, that these newer church movements do not begin to go down the arrogant road of anti-Semitism.

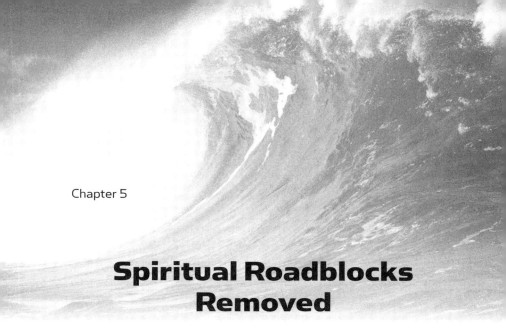

Chapter 5

Spiritual Roadblocks Removed

ISRAEL WAS CHOSEN as an *example* nation by God—an older brother in His family. The Church has much to learn from God's dealings with Israel, both in a positive and negative sense. A shining example in obedience and a model of chastisement in disobedience, Israel remains a source of edification for those in the Church who have ears to hear and eyes to see.

> *Many people shall come and say, "Come, and let us go up to the mountain of the LORD, to the house of the God of Jacob; He will teach us His ways, and we shall walk in His paths.* **For out of Zion shall go forth the law, and the word of the LORD from Jerusalem"** (Isaiah 2:3).

A major theme in Paul's letter to the Romans is the tension between Jewish and Gentile believers in the Church. The apostle explains how God's grace is able to bring them together as one through salvation under a new covenant. In Paul's day, the Lord was just opening the door of salvation for the first time to the Gentiles. Paul understood that his ministry to non-Jews was the unfolding of a Bible mystery hidden in the heart of God for centuries. (See Ephesians 3:3-6, Romans 16:25-26.) What became known as the Christian Church grew out of Paul's and other apostles' ministries. Then, in the latter part of the twentieth century, God began turning back to the Jews. His purposes and dealings with the Jewish people have been misunderstood for nearly two thousand years. History has come full circle, and a foundational New Testament truth is being recovered. Jew and Gentile are meeting again in the Body of the Lord throughout the world. This is a return to a spiritual environment similar to the times when the New Testament was written. The recovery of these scriptural truths provides a spiritual and theological basis for the restoration of apostolic teaching in the Church.

Detours Around the Cross

There are two misinterpretations of Scripture on either side of God's biblical revelation for Israel. Each error seeks in a different way to circumvent God's intention to complete His redemptive work in all nations by making Israel a living example once again. Each of the two errors defines a path around the altar of Jesus' sacrificial death on the Cross rather than directly to the altar and into resurrection and new life. God's will is for Jew and Gentile, secure in their respective identities, to be joined as one through the Lord's sacrifice on the Cross. Paul the Apostle wrote:

> *For He Himself is our peace, who has made both one, and has broken down the middle wall of separation, having abolished in His flesh the enmity, that is, the law of commandments contained in ordinances, so as to create in Himself one new man from the two, thus making peace, and that He might **reconcile them both***

to God in one body through the cross, thereby putting to death the enmity (Ephesians 2:14-16).

Replacement Theology

There are some Gentile Christians who teach that God no longer sees any special significance in Israel or His original covenant people, the Jews. Among the Scriptures that are used to support this view is the parable told by Jesus found in Luke, chapter 20. Jesus describes the dilemma of a man who planted a vineyard, rented it out to vine-growers, and then went on a journey for a long time. The owner sent three slaves, and each requested his rightful payment. The slaves were mistreated, and finally, the owner sent his own son. When the vine-growers saw the son, they said, "This is the heir; let's kill him and take his inheritance." So they took him out of the vineyard and killed him. Finishing this parable, Jesus said, *"Therefore what will the owner of the vineyard do to them? He will come and destroy those vine-growers and give the vineyard to others"* (Luke 20:15-16). This same parable, recorded in Matthew's gospel, is followed by Jesus saying, *"Therefore I say to you, the kingdom of God will be taken from you and given to a nation* [Greek: *ethne* or "people"] *bearing the fruits of it"* (Matthew 21:43).

These passages have been used to show that God intended to take His kingdom away from the Jews and give it to the Gentile Church. Jesus' words indicate that God would indeed give His kingdom to others, but to whom did Jesus say God would give the kingdom? God's kingdom was not taken from Israel and given exclusively to Gentile Christians. God took the priestly administration of His kingdom from the Levitical priesthood and gave it to Jesus and His own personally trained Jewish disciples. Jesus told His disciples, *"Do not fear, little flock, for it is your Father's good pleasure to give you the kingdom"* (Luke 12:32). These loyal friends of Jesus were the ones He knew would follow Him to the Cross—and beyond.

It was to the disciple Peter, a Jewish fisherman from the Galilee, that Jesus gave the "keys of the kingdom of heaven." After Jesus' ascension, Peter used these kingdom "keys" to open the doors of the kingdom to Gentiles at the home of Cornelius in Caesarea. According to the Book of Acts, the Messianic Jewish leaders in Jerusalem were at first shocked to hear of Peter's actions. When he explained carefully to them how God had led him, *"They quieted down and glorified God, saying, 'Well then, God has granted to the Gentiles also the repentance that leads to life'"* (Acts 11:18, NASB). The key words are "to the Gentiles also," meaning *with* the Messianic Jews, not in place of them. Gentiles were added to the original Jewish disciples, sharing in their inheritance, but not replacing them.

Dual Covenant Theology

The other error that parallels replacement theology is the belief that God's covenants with the Jewish people exempt them from accepting Jesus as the only means of salvation. It is argued that since God's commandments and promises to Moses were everlasting, they were not broken or abolished in order to institute another covenant. However, the purpose of all God's covenants with humankind since the fall has been redemption. God's acts of redemption find their culmination in the person of His Son and chosen Redeemer, Jesus. God therefore, did not break His previous covenants with Israel, but rather He fulfilled them redemptively in the provision of His Son.

Dual covenant theology says that the Law is sufficient for the Jewish people, and Jesus' redemption through the Cross is only for the Gentiles. However, Jesus made the way of salvation clear to His own Jewish disciples when He said to them, *"I am the way, and the truth, and the life. No one comes to the Father, except through Me"* (John 14:6). Nicodemus was a respected leader in the Jewish community, but Jesus told him that he needed to be "born again" to see the Kingdom of God. The Apostle Peter stood up on the day of Pentecost and boldly proclaimed the name of Jesus to his almost completely Jewish audience. Peter said, *"Therefore let all the house of Israel know assuredly that God has made this Jesus, whom you crucified, both Lord and Christ"* (Acts 2:36). The writer of Acts goes on to record the following:

> *Now when they heard this, they were cut to the heart, and said to Peter and the rest of the apostles, "Men and brethren, what shall we do?" Then Peter said to them, "Repent, and let every one of you be baptized in the name of Jesus Christ for the remission of sins; and you shall receive the gift of the Holy Spirit"* (*Acts* 2:37-38).

If the Jewish crowd that was gathered in Jerusalem needed only the law for salvation, why did Peter exhort them to repent and be baptized in the name of Jesus the Messiah? Paul's cry for the salvation of the Jewish people reveals a similar understanding. Far from exhorting his own people to rely on the law for their righteousness and salvation, Paul wrote:

> *Brethren, my heart's desire and prayer to God for Israel is that they may be saved. For I bear them witness that they have a zeal for God, but not according to knowledge. For they being ignorant of God's righteousness, and seeking to establish their own righteousness, have not submitted to the righteousness of God. For Christ is the end of the law for righteousness to everyone who believes* (Romans 10:1-4).

In this passage of Scripture, the Greek word translated "end" is *telos*, which is defined as the goal, completion, or perfection of something. This means that the revelation of Jesus as Messiah is the goal, fulfillment, and completion of Israel's divine, unbreakable, covenant law.

Restoring the Roman Road

Modern history has had a profound impact on Christian thinking. In 1948, Israel was re-established as a modern nation. In the mid-1960s, Messianic Jews began to emerge as identifiable members of the Lord's Body. Now, for the first time in nearly twenty centuries, when we read "Israel" in the Scriptures (particularly the Apostle Paul's writings in the New Testament), we can know it simply means the Jewish nation. We don't need to spiritualize or allegorize that word to get its basic meaning for today. Similarly, when Paul's writings contain references to Jews in the Church, we understand that he is writing about Messianic Jews. Several chapters in Paul's writings (see Romans 11, Galatians 3, Ephesians 2, Colossians 3) address the issue of unity between Jews and Gentiles in the Church. Now we can read these New Testament letters as if they were written just for us.

Today, we realize that the whole letter to the Romans is in a single flow of the Spirit, speaking directly to Jew and Gentile. Now, with this understanding, the book reads smoothly all the way through with valuable revelation in every chapter. The final chapters contain powerful apostolic instructions for the Church that are built upon the flow of Paul's arguments in the earlier chapters. The Apostle Paul's gospel and the fullness of its message are being restored to the Church in these last days. God is removing the "roadblock" of Romans, chapters 9 through 11. When Paul was writing (or dictating) the Roman letter, he was ministering a single, integrated revelation of the Holy Spirit. In the final verses at the end of chapter 11, the apostle actually sings a song of praise to God. But he is not finished with the letter. Without a break, we can now move from chapter 11 to the altar of personal sacrifice discussed in chapter 12, verses 1 and 2, and then beyond into the apostolic instructions of the closing chapters.

Christians regard the New Testament Scriptures to be the inspired Word of God. But what is inspired about these words?

Is the inspiration in what we think the words mean centuries after they were written, or in what the inspired writer was thinking at the time when he received the words from the Holy Spirit? Of course, it is the latter. This means the closer you and I can *sit* to the Apostle Paul and understand his concerns and his worldview, the closer we are to his inspiration and the meaning of God's words. When Paul wrote Romans, Israel was still the nation of the Jews and there were many Jewish believers in the churches. Now that these facts are being restored, we have a chance to sit closer to Paul than any previous generation of Christians in nearly 2000 years. This restoration is a clear preparation for the end-times and the Bride-like Church of Jew and Gentile that will welcome Jesus when He returns to Israel as Messiah and King.

Most Christians today would say that the really important verses in the letter to the Romans are to be found in the first eight chapters. Few people memorize verses from the final chapters. However, now the whole apostolic gospel contained in Romans is being restored to the Church so that there will be solid, scriptural foundations for the restoration of apostolic authority in the Church worldwide. This is an essential aspect of God's plan to restore His biblical revelation to the Church in the end-times. Using Israel as His instrument, the Holy Spirit is stirring church leaders to recover the Jewish roots of their faith. The Old Testament is coming alive again to many Gentile Christians, and interest in biblical Hebrew is growing in churches around the world. Ministries that seek to penetrate secular society and reclaim the marketplace, education system, or government are rooted in the Hebraic concept that every God-given vocation is holy. The Church's current interest in Israel and prayer for Jewish people is much more than blowing a *shofar*, wearing a prayer shawl, and praying the Aaronic benediction in Hebrew. It is a manifestation of a broader understanding of the Bible, and God is requiring this understanding to meet the challenges of our generation. *"Faith comes by hearing and hearing by the word of*

God" (Romans 10:17). How can the faith of the Church grow without having stronger and deeper biblical foundations in the Old Testament as well as in the New? How can there be a modern prophetic movement without accurate alignment to the biblical prophecies provided by Israel's resurrection as a nation? Similarly, an end-time apostolic movement will be severely limited without fully recovering the inspired, apostolic worldview of Paul's letters. Understanding, by revelation, the significance of Israel, and the nations is a key to this recovery.

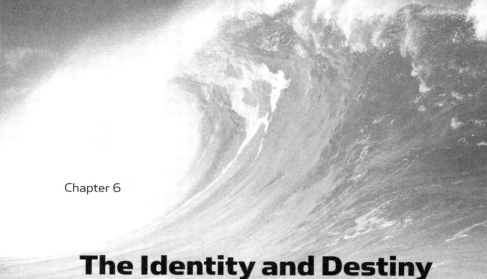

Chapter 6

The Identity and Destiny of Islam

WE ARE FACING TURBULENT AND DANGEROUS TIMES, not only here in Israel, but around the world. At the core of the turbulence, there is a bitter hatred for Israel and the Jewish people. In 2002, Daniel Pearl, an American journalist for the *Wall Street Journal*, was brutally murdered in Pakistan after he was made to say, "I am a Jew and my mother is a Jew." Suicide bombings used to be rare outside of the Israeli-Palestinian conflict, but now are spreading around the world. In the most recent Palestinian *intifada* (uprising), which began at the end of September 2000, over one thousand Israelis have been killed and thousands more wounded. Other recent bombings in Bali and Djakarta (Indonesia), Mombasa (Kenya), Davao City (Philippines), Mumbai (India), Casablanca (Morocco), and Riyadh (Saudi Arabia), as well as throughout Iraq and Afghanistan, have claimed hundreds of lives. In Kenya, the target of the bombing was an Israeli-owned hotel filled with Israeli tourists. In Casablanca (May 2003), the targets were a Jewish Community Center and other sites frequented by Jews.

The origin of Arab/Islamic hatred of Israel and the West, the United States in particular, is rooted in spiritual conflict, but it also has important human elements. We must learn to understand the roots of this hatred if we are to combat the spirit that drives it. The Lord commands us to love our enemies and pray for those who hurt us. How can we love and pray for those whose hearts we cannot comprehend? Understanding spiritual rejection is the most important factor in getting to the root of Islamic hatred and terrorism. Rejection is something that we all experience. Rejection means not being chosen, favored, or blessed. Rejection hurts and can leave lasting damage, especially when it comes at the hand of someone close—a brother or sister, a parent, a pastor, a good friend, a spouse or someone you wanted to marry. Jesus knows how it feels. He was rejected, too. John, the disciple of Jesus, wrote, *"He came to His own, and His own did not receive Him"* (John 1:11). Isaiah, the prophet wrote concerning God's suffering servant, the Messiah, *"He was despised and rejected by men, a man of sorrows and acquainted with grief"* (Isaiah 53:3a).

Rejection can wound so deeply that, as a means of defense, those who are deeply hurt will deny that they have been rejected. Denial does not heal the wound, but distracts attention from otherwise intolerable pain. The dynamics of that woundedness then continue to exist beneath the surface. It is important to recognize the hurt of rejection, confront denial, and apply God's cure for the wound. There is deep spiritual rejection and denial that have caused a resistance to healing for centuries in the Middle East. This chapter will examine the Arab-Israeli conflict through biblical, prophetic glasses in order to see the wound of rejection and the sinful reactions it has produced over the generations. Then, we can focus on God's solution.

The Rejected Brother

God is a sovereign King. He is the Everlasting Father who makes crucial decisions and choices that affect us all. The Bible itself is a record of God's choices and how they define His purposes in Heaven and on Earth. Under the inspiration of the Holy Spirit, the prophet Malachi wrote about one of God's key choices:

> *"I have loved you," says the LORD. "Yet you say, 'In what way have You loved us?' Was not Esau Jacob's brother?" says the LORD, "Yet Jacob I have loved; but Esau I have hated...."* (Malachi 1:2-3a).

The Apostle Paul quotes these same verses in his letter to the Romans: *As it is written, "Jacob I have loved, but Esau I have hated." What shall we say then? Is there unrighteousness with God? Certainly not! For He says to Moses, "I will have mercy on whomever I will have mercy, and I will have compassion on whomever I will have compassion"* (Romans 9:13-15).

Scripture teaches that God chose Jacob instead of his older brother Esau, even before they were born. God's choice of Jacob was therefore sovereign, and was based on His perfect foreknowledge rather than on the behavior of either of the brothers. In biblical language, the term "love" refers more to actions than feelings. God chose to relate to Jacob in love. His hatred toward Esau was not necessarily an emotional hatred, but rather the choice not to relate to him with the same intimacy as with Jacob. By God's decision, Abraham's inheritance which was passed on to his son Isaac, was given in turn to his grandson, Jacob. God rejected Esau, and he was excluded from the chosen family line.

As students of the Bible, our usual emphasis is on the life and spiritual condition of the chosen son. We tend to follow the redemptive lineage. We all know the stories of Abraham, Isaac, and Jacob (later renamed Israel). Jacob's sons became the heads of the twelve tribes of Israel. From the twelve tribes came Moses and the judges, all the prophets and the kings, even Jesus and the apostles. What happened to the rejected side of the family? The rejected son, Esau, had a wounded heart. Esau turned to bitterness, jealousy, and murderous anger. This is simply an example of fallen human nature.

The Bible records similar patterns of events from the beginning of human history. Both sons of Adam and Eve brought offerings to God, but God accepted the offering of only one brother, Abel. Cain's offering was rejected. Cain tried to solve the problem of his rejection by hating his brother Abel. He was overcome with jealousy because his brother had found God's favor, and eventually Cain murdered Abel. Generations later, God made a choice among the twelve sons of Israel and chose Joseph for a special destiny. The other brothers hated Joseph and plotted to kill him. Esau was no different in nurturing hatred toward his younger brother, Jacob.

So Esau hated Jacob because of the blessing with which his father blessed him, and Esau said in his heart, "The days of mourning for my father are at hand; then I will kill my brother Jacob" (Genesis 27:41).

Previously, Esau had chosen wives that displeased his parents. Now, desperate to recover the blessing he had lost, Esau sought to marry a woman he thought would be acceptable.

Esau saw that Isaac had blessed Jacob and sent him away to Padan Aram to take himself a wife from there, and that as he blessed him he gave him a charge, saying, "You shall not take a wife from the daughters of Canaan," and that Jacob had obeyed his father and his mother and had gone to Padan Aram. Also Esau saw that the daughters of Canaan did not please his father

Isaac. So Esau went to Ishmael and took Mahalath the daughter of Ishmael, Abraham's son, the sister of Nebajoth, to be his wife in addition to the wives he had (Genesis 28:6-9).

Thus, Esau married into the family of Ishmael. Who was Ishmael? He was another rejected brother from a generation earlier. Ishmael was the older half brother of Isaac. God chose Isaac, and then told Isaac's father Abraham to send Ishmael and his mother Hagar away. A promise to become a strong nation was given to Ishmael, but God rejected him as part of the chosen, redemptive lineage. So when Esau married Ishmael's eldest daughter, the family lines were joined.

The spiritual identity of Esau and his descendants is known as "Edom." This word in Hebrew means "red," and it comes from the red stew that Jacob made and sold to Esau for his birthright.

> *Now Jacob cooked a stew; and Esau came in from the field, and he was weary. And Esau said to Jacob, "Please feed me with that same red stew, for I am weary."* **Therefore his name was called Edom.** *But Jacob said, "Sell me your birthright as of this day"* (Genesis 25:29-31).

Consider the feelings of a people group whose very name relates to a shameful event in the life of their forefather. How do they explain the origin and meaning of their own name? How should they deal with the collective hurt of rejection as well as their anger against the descendants of Jacob, the brother who deceived and superseded their patriarch? Jacob, who became known as Israel, inherited the land given by God to his grandfather, Abraham. It became known as the land of Israel. Since the days of the Bible, this inheritance—the land of

Israel—has been viewed by the people of Edom as rightfully theirs.

Islam Is Denial

The spiritual dynamics of rejection can lead to a broken heart, humility, forgiveness, and healing or it can lead to anger, hostility, defensiveness, and denial. The people of Edom chose the latter. Edom is no longer used as their name, and over the centuries, they and the other descendants of Ishmael and Esau developed another faith and another book they consider holy. This faith is called Islam, and their book, the Koran, contradicts the Bible at key points in the historical record. The Koran teaches that it was not Isaac that Abraham took to the mountain of sacrifice, but Ishmael. The Koran teaches that Allah, the god of Islam, has no son. The Koran denies the rejection that Edom and Ishmael have experienced because of God's choices. It could be said that the Koran exists in order to contradict the Bible. The strength of Islam lies in its outright denial of the biblical record.

Who are the descendants of Edom, and where do they live today? According to the Bible, Esau lived in Mount Seir, which is in southern Jordan at the head of the Arabian Peninsula. The people of Edom (along with the descendants of Ishmael and other rejected sons of Abraham) are the people of Arabia, Jordan, and the surrounding area. They are the Arab people. Genesis 36:8 states, *"So Esau dwelt in Mount Seir. Esau is Edom."*

We should now understand why the Arab people so vehemently object to the Jewish people returning to the land that was promised to Abraham. This land is the disputed inheritance, and the conflict between Arabs and Jews over the land is the longest-running family feud in the history of the world. The very presence of the Jewish people in their ancient land reawakens ancient spirits of jealousy and bitterness. The Bible says this spirit of Edom cries out for the complete destruction of Israel, so that the memory of Israel (and the pain of rejection) will be removed forever.

> *Do not keep silent, O God! Do not hold Your peace and do not be still, O God! For behold, Your enemies make a tumult; and t**hose who hate You have lifted up their head**. They have taken crafty counsel against Your people, and consulted together against Your sheltered ones. **They have said, "Come, and let us cut them off from being a nation, that the name of Israel may be remembered no more.**" For they have consulted together with one consent; they form a confederacy against You: **the tents of Edom and the Ishmaelites**; Moab and the Hagrites; Gebal, Ammon, and Amalek; Philistia with the inhabitants of Tyre; Assyria also has joined with them. They have helped the children of Lot. Selah* (Psalm 83:1-8).

God's Healing for Rejection

The old saying, "Time heals all wounds," is simply not true. It is not the passage of time, but rather the decision to forgive that starts the healing process. The wound of rejection cannot be healed until the wounded ones recognize their need for healing and their need to forgive. Denial of the wound prevents healing and reconciliation from becoming a reality. How does God, a loving Father to all humankind, deal with denial? In His love and concern for every human, God acts to confront it. In the rest of the verses of Psalm 83, the writer cries out to God to confront the people and spirit of Edom, for the purpose of revealing the truth to them.

> *Deal with them* *as with Midian, as with Sisera, as with Jabin at the Brook Kishon, who perished at En Dor, who became as refuse on the earth. Make their nobles like Oreb and like Zeeb, yes, all their princes like Zebah*

*and Zalmunna, who said, "Let us take for ourselves the pastures of God for a possession." ... Fill their faces with shame, **that they may seek Your name, O LORD.** Let them be confounded and dismayed forever; yes, let them be put to shame and perish, **that they may know that You, whose name alone is the LORD, are the Most High over all the earth** (Psalm 83: 9-12, 16-18).*

Every one of us has experienced the pain of rejection. We can understand what it feels like to be passed over, to not be chosen, blessed, or favored. When we experience difficult things in life—the loss of a job, death of a family member or loved one, the rebellion of a spouse or child—it can seem that we have been rejected by God. Sometimes, we compare our lives with others and feel it is unfair that we should be marked for hardship or sorrow. Some of us have never experienced the love of a warm and accepting family environment. Being rejected by mother or father can produce long-term wounds and character problems that are stubbornly resistant to prayer and counseling. How can each of us receive healing for wounds of rejection, and then glorify God most fully in our lives?

The Bible states that God has only one Son who has been with Him since before the beginning of time. This Son, Jesus, has all the favor and acceptance that God the Father has to offer. Jesus has received from His Father all authority and power both in Heaven and on Earth. When we accept Jesus as Lord and give Him our lives, we become a part of His body. Even if you have been rejected throughout your life, in Him there is not only acceptance from the Father, but all the fullness of God himself. In Jesus, every believer is accepted in love and granted the rights and privileges of a chosen child of God. This is our spiritual inheritance.

Paul wrote the following to believers in Ephesus and Colosse:

> *Blessed be the God and Father of our Lord Jesus Christ, who has blessed us with every spiritual blessing in the heavenly places in Christ, just as **He chose us in Him before the foundation of the world, that we should be holy and without blame before Him in love, having predestined us to adoption as sons** by Jesus Christ to Himself, according to the good pleasure of His will, to the praise of the glory of His grace, by which **He has made us accepted in the Beloved**. In Him we have redemption through His blood, the forgiveness of sins, according to the riches of His grace* (Ephesians 1:3-7).

> *For in Him dwells all the fullness of the Godhead bodily; and **you are complete in Him**, who is the head of all principality and power* (Colossians 2:9-10).

God makes choices, and we must choose to be in agreement with His will. Often God will choose others for blessing, and we may feel abandoned for a season. So often when others are honored, we feel dishonored in comparison. When painful things happen in our lives, we may think that God is choosing to ignore us. We can either turn to bitterness and anger or we can choose life in the Messiah. If we join with Jesus and come before God "in Him," we will find the ultimate acceptance and healing for our rejected hearts. This is God's way. God's own sovereign choices often result in someone being rejected. However, God has provided for every person to be accepted and fully healed through His own Son, Jesus.

Reconciliation of Brothers

In the biblical narrative, Jacob and Esau meet again many years later. After Jacob fled from his brother's wrath, the day came when he could no longer avoid facing his older sibling. However, Jacob had been changed by his years of labor and by wrestling with God. Also, something had happened in Esau's heart during the intervening years. Esau had been transformed into a man at peace with his brother by a work of God's grace. Even though the people of Esau are still at war with the descendants of Jacob, this biblical story is a prophetic picture of reconciliation that is yet to come between Jew and Arab.

> *Now Jacob lifted his eyes and looked, and there, Esau was coming, and with him were four hundred men. So he divided the children among Leah, Rachel, and the two maidservants. And he put the maidservants and their children in front, Leah and her children behind, and Rachel and Joseph last. Then he crossed over before them and bowed himself to the ground seven times, until he came near to his brother.* **But Esau ran to meet him, and embraced him, and fell on his neck and kissed him, and they wept.** *And he lifted his eyes and saw the women and children, and said, "Who are these with you?" And he said, "The children whom God has graciously given your servant." Then the maidservants came near, they and their children, and bowed down. And Leah also came near with her children, and they bowed down. Afterward Joseph and Rachel came near, and they bowed down. Then Esau said, "What do you mean by all this company which I met?" And he said, "These are to find favor in the sight of my lord." But* **Esau said, "I have enough, my brother; keep what you have for yourself."** *And Jacob said, "No, please, if I have now found favor in your sight, then receive my present from my hand, inasmuch as I* **have seen your face as though I had seen the face of God,** *and you were pleased with me"* (Genesis 33:1-10).

These passages in Genesis depict a humble Jacob and an Esau whose hatred and anger have been miraculously wiped away. Esau says, "I have enough, my brother." His heart has been satisfied and his bitterness at the loss of his birthright is gone. He embraces his brother with love and kindness. This is a prophetic picture of born-again Arabs—former Muslims—coming with the love of Jesus to unredeemed Israel. These sons of Ishmael and Esau will be healed of deep rejection. Their bitterness and hatred will be melted away by the fire of God's Spirit in their hearts. Israel's greatest enemies will come, not to take Jewish lives, but to lay down their own lives so that the Jews may know their Messiah. These are the born-again descendants of Ishmael and Esau who will proclaim the "fullness of the Gentiles" to Israel (See Romans 11:25.), and who will provoke the Jewish people to jealousy (See Romans 11:11).

Jealousy is different from envy. Envy is wanting what belongs to someone else. Jealousy is aroused when someone else has what is rightfully yours. Jesus, the Messiah, is the "King of the Jews." The gospel of salvation is to "the Jew first and also to the Gentile." (See Romans 1:16).When the Jewish people see the blessings of their Messiah on the other (rejected) side of Abraham's family, they will be provoked to a spiritual jealousy that will attract them to the Lord. When Jacob experienced love from Esau, it is recorded in the book of Genesis that he said, *"I have seen your face as though I had seen the face of God"*! The gospel of Jesus Christ and revival in the Middle East are God's answers to war between Arabs and Jews. This is the hope that God provides—when the Prince of Peace rules on both sides of Abraham's family, there will be genuine peace in the Middle East.

Chapter 7

Tsunami!

IT WAS ALREADY HOT inside the little room. Old paint was peeling from the concrete walls. An electric fan was whirring, but doing no more than moving the stale air from one side of the room to the other. People were all around me, kneeling on the hard floor, praying in Chinese. We had been like this for more than an hour and it was still early in the morning. Impassioned prayers burst forth from faces contorted with intense concentration. Arms were raised and tears began to flow. Soon the floor was littered with damp facial tissues. I was in a secret location somewhere in an industrial suburb of Beijing, and another day had begun with the underground family church movement.

Later that day, I sat with the "First Uncle" or leader of the group that had invited me. This man in his sixties led a network of house churches comprising more than two million people. He said that he had been in prison recently, but that things were a little better now. Through the interpreter, I understood he meant that there was less torture and fewer executions of church leaders than in the days of the Cultural Revolution. "We pray for the communist government of China," he said. "We pray that God will change their hearts toward the gospel."

The First Uncle had a great interest in Israel, and he told me that members of his movement wanted to bring God's good news to the Jewish people. He understood that the Messiah will be returning to the land of Israel, and that Chinese Christians have a role to play in bringing the gospel across Asia to Jerusalem. During my visit with the First Uncle and his group of leaders, I spoke to them about the prophetic significance of modern Israel. The purity of their hunger for God's Word was refreshing and an encouragement to me as their teacher. They were young people, most of them only in their twenties. I was greatly impressed by their commitment, simple faith, and their desire to serve the Lord despite humble circumstances and in the face of real persecution.

Later in my visit, a Korean missionary arrived with his young interpreter. This missionary said that he had been working for years bringing Chinese Bibles (printed in Korea) to groups all over China. We both marveled at God's amazing work in China. Reportedly, the present revival of Christian faith has been growing for an entire generation at an estimated average rate of more than twenty thousand new believers a day. We spoke about the Silk Road, a network of ancient trade routes linking China with the Middle East. Centuries ago, the gospel may have first come to China along this route from the land of Israel. Today, however, Asian Christians are using this route again to bring the Bible's message back across the continent through Central Asia. Their ultimate goal is the Middle East and Jerusalem.

Months after my visit to Beijing, I sat with a man in Singapore who is a *watchman* for the house church movement in Mainland China. It was he who had connected me with the First Uncle and his group. "The house church movement is comprised of many different streams or separate networks of believers in China," he said. "However, there are a few main groups that are all led by men who began as young itinerant

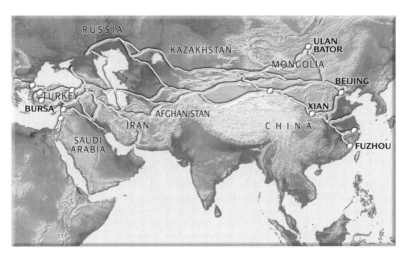

The Silk Road from China to the Middle East

evangelists during the time of the Cultural Revolution. These men have spent years in prison for their faith, and now their groups are quite large." "How large?" I asked. "Well, if you use conservative figures, the estimate for just these main groups is about fifty to seventy million people," said the watchman. "They have begun meeting together as leaders to pray about God's purpose in creating greater unity among their movements. They believe God is leading them to begin to send the gospel to other nations. Their vision is to send one hundred thousand preachers, teachers, and church planters. The code name they have chosen for this unity movement is *Sinim*."

I knew this word, *Sinim*. It has the same meaning in the Modern Hebrew language that it did in the days of the Bible. If you eat Chinese food in Israel, you go to eat *ochel sini* (pronounced see-nee). The word for China is *Sin* (pronounced like the English word "seen"), and the Chinese people are *Sinim* (seen-eem). This word is found exactly once in the Hebrew Bible, in the 49th chapter of the book of the prophet Isaiah.

*I will make each of My mountains a road, and My highways shall be elevated. Surely these shall come from afar; Look! Those from the north and the west, **and these from the land of Sinim*** (Isaiah 49:11-12).

These inspired, prophetic Scriptures speak of a gathering of God's people to the land of Israel from all directions including the nation of China. Moreover, this gathering is connected to God's restoration of Israel as a nation. The prophet speaks about the establishment of a spiritual "highway" that will provide guidance for God's people concerning His purposes. Yes, I knew Isaiah chapter 49 well. Years earlier God had given me a vision of a spiritual bridge or highway linking Israel with His mighty work in East Asia.

Why is today's great Christian movement in China so significant? Surely, there have been other large revivals of Christianity in different parts of the world. Is there some reason why a contemporary Christian movement spanning East Asia has special relevance to God's end-time plan? The answer is that this movement is not only massive in terms of numbers, but it is historic. The Bible's message has never before had such deep and widespread impact in East Asia. If the recent, phenomenal growth of the Church in South Korea and other places like the Philippines, Singapore, Indonesia, and Malaysia are added to what is being seen in China today, an incredible picture emerges. We are not looking at a steadily rising tide, but rather at a tidal wave of first-generation church growth.

Welcome to the Pacific Century

The rise of modern Asia as a great economic and political power and the explosive church growth in this region began about the same time as the re-establishment of the State of Israel. After the end of World War II and the Korean War, the Church in Korea, which had grown slowly in the past, began to move into revival and an unprecedented surge in numerical growth. In 1958, a young Bible school graduate named Yong-Gi Cho founded a small tent church in the outskirts of Seoul. Made of hand-sewn fragments of army tents for a roof and straw mats for a floor, the church, which began with only five members, soon became a beacon of hope in war-ravaged South Korea. By 1962, the congregation had increased to eight hundred. Eleven years later in 1973, the membership reached ten thousand. Based on fervent prayer and faith in a prayer-answering God, the Yoido Full Gospel Church also pioneered the home cell-group movement. By delegating frontline pastoral and evangelistic responsibilities to thousands of lay ministers in their own neighborhoods, Dr. Cho kept his huge church small and local. The Yoido Full Gospel Church is associated with the Assemblies of God, a Pentecostal denomination that began in America. Today, with a membership of more than seven hundred thousand people, this church has set a precedent as the largest single congregation, Protestant or Catholic, in Church history.

I met Dr. Cho in 1980, while I was a seminary student in southern California. He had come to speak at a Christian convention nearby, and I volunteered to be his driver. For a week, I took him to meetings, back and forth from his hotel. In the process, I got to know this gifted and unusual man. Apart from being a spiritually powerful servant of the Lord, I found him to be down-to-earth, very approachable, and able to laugh at himself. At the time, his church in Seoul had just exceeded one hundred thousand in attendance, and Dr. Cho had a heart to share what God was doing in Korea. My wife and I were preparing to launch out in ministry to Japan. He encouraged me to visit the new World Mission Center that was built next to the huge sanctuary where the congregation met on Yoido Island. I saw him again when my own pastor invited me to share the platform at the All Japan Pentecostal Ministers' Fellowship held in Ise, Japan, in 1981. Dr. Cho preached in the Japanese language and was ministering in faith for a great revival in Japan. We kept in touch over the years, and today, I serve on the board of directors for Church Growth International (CGI), an organization of church leaders from around the world. Dr. Cho began CGI in 1976, to promote church growth through leadership training, prayer, and the impartation of faith and vision.

The Yoido Full Gospel Church is not alone in proving that record church growth is now an Asian phenomenon. Presbyterianism began in Scotland in the seventeenth century, but today the largest and most dynamic Presbyterian congregations in the world are all found in South Korea. Methodism traces it origins back to the preaching of John Wesley, and this movement began with groups of students at Oxford University in the late 1720s. Today, the largest Methodist congregations in the world are in Seoul. In Singapore and Malaysia, it is not uncommon to find congregations numbering in the thousands and even tens of thousands. Evangelical churches in other Asian countries like Indonesia, India, and the Philippines are growing at an amazing rate. Churches are growing in Thailand, Vietnam, and Cambodia, countries in which there has never been a widespread movement toward the gospel. Almost all of this sudden growth has taken place since the 1950s.

In roughly the same fifty-year period, Japan, the only nation to be attacked with atom bombs, rose from the ashes of defeat to become an engine of economic growth for the entire region. From near starvation after the devastation of World War II, Japan grew to become the world's second largest economy. The "Land of the Rising Sun" at the eastern edge of Asia became the world's leader in high quality manufacturing. Japan has already set an example for the emerging Asian *tiger* economies, such as Korea, Taiwan, Hong Kong, and Singapore. Now, with the opening and the rapid growth of the massive mainland Chinese market, many agree that the world's economic direction in the twenty-first century will be decided in Asia. Seven out of the ten largest urban populations are Asian, and a growing portion of the world's total economic output comes from Asia. Even periods of severe financial turmoil in Asia have been instrumental in promoting reform of corrupt and outmoded systems. This will ultimately strengthen the long-term prospects for Asian economic growth.

Historically, in many nations where the gospel has taken root and grown, far-reaching, positive social change has occurred, along with increased prosperity and political might. Today, for the first time in history, one sees nations in East Asia becoming politically powerful and affluent while millions embrace true Christian faith. Why has God chosen to visit Asia with these blessings and challenges at this particular time? Is this just an accident of history? I was born in the United States, but moved to Japan with my parents when I was ten years old in 1961. That is not so long ago, but it was a different Asia then. I remember when the phrase, "made in Japan," meant cheap, low quality products. We lived in Thailand during the early 1970s when there were water buffalos still plowing rice paddies along the two-lane highway to the old Bangkok airport. Now, that road is a raised super-highway with high-rise office buildings along most of the route. Bangkok's newest international airport is a huge, modern complex jammed with thousands of visitors from virtually everywhere in the world. I also remember the days when Singapore was a quiet little seaside town with a quaint, British colonial flavor. Today, Singapore's harbor is the busiest container port in the world, and the per capita income there is higher than in England. Korea was devastated by war in the 1950s. Seoul was a burnt out, war-ravaged landscape. Now, when you look across the city of Seoul at night, you will see a skyline glowing with light and color. The city is filled with modern buildings and crowded with churches. Some city blocks have more than one church, and many display red neon crosses on their roofs. This phenomenal growth is clearly the blessing of God.

What is His purpose in building up Asia today and in what direction is He going?

Around the World From East to West

For as the lightning comes from the east and flashes to the west, so also will the coming of the Son of Man be (Matthew 24:27).

A very brief overview of the movement of the gospel since its earliest days shows what happens when its influence becomes firmly rooted in culture. Since the early days of the Book of Acts, the gospel has expanded in a westward direction. It is written in the sixteenth chapter of Acts that while in present-day Turkey, Paul wanted to go east and preach the Word of God in Asia. Twice it is recorded that God redirected him. Luke, the author of the Book of Acts, wrote the following:

> *Now when they had gone through Phrygia and the region of Galatia, **they were forbidden by the Holy Spirit to preach the word in Asia**. After they had come to Mysia, **they tried to go into Bithynia, but the Spirit did not permit them**. So passing by Mysia, they came down to Troas. And a vision appeared to Paul in the night. A man of Macedonia stood and pleaded with him, saying, "Come over to Macedonia and help us." Now after he had seen the vision, immediately we sought to go to Macedonia, concluding that the Lord had called us to preach the gospel to them* (Acts 16:6-10).

This portion of Acts, chapter 16, is an account of Paul's second missionary journey. He was traveling with Silas (a believer from Jerusalem), Timothy (Paul's young Jewish disciple), and Luke (a Gentile doctor). They left Jerusalem and launched out into the area that is now southern Turkey to preach the gospel and strengthen the existing churches. Paul had grown up in this area. He knew the territory, the language, and the culture. It would have been natural for him to continue evangelizing in Asia Minor, but the Lord had other plans. They were "forbidden by the Holy Spirit to preach the word in Asia," a phrase that sounds as if they were given a prophetic word of guidance. They then tried to go north to Bithynia, but again they received supernatural guidance that directed them another way. This apostolic team had come from the south. They were prevented from going east or north. The only way available to them was west. So west they went, until they reached the coast at a place called Troas (the site of ancient Troy).

In Troas, they must have prayed and probably fasted for God's guidance. Today, we would probably do the same while faxing or emailing our intercessors back home for prayer support. God answered them, and Paul received a nighttime vision of a Macedonian man calling out to them for help. Luke records that they immediately knew it was guidance from God, and they prepared to cross over into Macedonia. This may be one of the most significant moments in the history of the Church in terms of its geographical expansion. It was a decisive move since Troas is on the Asian continent, and Macedonia is in Europe. Up until then, the gospel had been a purely Asian phenomenon. It did not remain that way. God's purpose was for the gospel to go west into Europe. The gospel has been traveling steadily westward ever since that time, even to this day.

Paul's team responded to the vision and crossed over into Macedonia and Greece, bringing the gospel into Europe. This is one of the reasons why the New Testament was originally written in Greek rather than in Arabic or in the language of a people to the east of Israel. Much of the New Testament is in the form of inspired letters written to churches in European cities—Philippi, Corinth, Thessalonica, and Rome. In his letter written to the Romans years later, Paul showed he fully understood the Lord's strategic westward direction for the gospel. He told the Roman church that he had fully preached the gospel from Jerusalem as far west as Illyricum on the Adriatic Sea (modern Albania). Paul wrote, *"Whenever I journey to Spain, I shall come to you ... Therefore, when I have performed this and have sealed to them this fruit, I shall go by way of you to Spain"* (Romans 15:24a and 28a).

From Jerusalem, Spain is as far west as one can go before facing the mighty Atlantic Ocean. More than fourteen hundred years before Columbus, Spain must have seemed like the end of the world. However, that is exactly the direction the gospel took in the years following the journeys of the Apostle Paul. Rome was as far as Paul's ministry took him, but the gospel had been successfully launched into the West. The gospel saturated the Greek-speaking world and followed the Roman roads to the hub of the empire. In Rome, Christianity flourished and came into conflict with the official cult of emperor worship. For more than two centuries, the gospel fought a life and death battle with Roman culture. Visitors can still enter the catacombs where the early believers hid from persecution and buried their dead. The remains of the great coliseum still stand in Rome. It is the site where Christians were thrown to wild beasts as amusement for the pagans. The demonically inspired emperor Nero reportedly crucified Christians, coated their bodies with tar, and burned them as torches for his garden parties.

The Gospel in Europe

In the end, Rome weakened and fell, while the true believers in Jesus, both Jews and Gentiles stood strong. Rome became the victim of attacks by less civilized peoples from the north. The barbarians that sacked Rome were tribal groups like the Goths, Visigoths, Vandals, and the Huns. They were pagan peoples with their own mythologies and systems of primitive nature worship. History shows that they were gradually transformed by the Christian faith. These barbarians were the ancestors of the very civilized Swiss, Dutch, French, and Germans of today. The miracle of Christian Europe is that the local people began to believe the gospel that was totally foreign to them. Imagine convincing European pagans that a Middle Eastern holy man is the Son of God and must be worshipped and served. Most of them had never even heard of Israel and the Jewish people before. Even though faith in a Jewish Messiah was completely foreign to Europe, Christianity moved like a tidal wave across the continent, transforming whole nations and sinking down into the roots of European culture.

In time, Europeans began writing new laws for their society that were based on biblical principles. Christian art and architecture flourished. When a new town was built, the people wanted a house for God to be the central and most prominent building. Towering cathedrals, some that took over a century to build, began marking cities from the Tiber to the Danube where paganism once reigned. Think of the faith that must have been in those believers to start building programs that their grandchildren would finish! In England, the preaching of the gospel turned the heart of the nation away from primitive, Stonehenge-like worship of the sun and moon and stars.

Centuries passed while Christian thought and biblical scholarship took root in Europe. Understanding of the one Creator God became the foundation of European power and cultural dominance by providing the key for scientific advancement. The first words you read in the Bible are, *"In the beginning God created the heavens and the earth"* (Genesis 1:1). Twenty-five verses later, the Bible says that God created humans to be like Him with dominion over every living thing. The secret of the European power is that it became a civilization that simply believed those words. Modern western science was founded upon the biblical revelation of a rational God who had created the universe and also created man in His own image. Because the early European scientists believed that the world was created by a God of reason, they knew that people created in His image could discover truth about nature through understanding. This Christian worldview became the basis for Europe's prosperity and political power through the spectacular success of modern science. It was not because European scientists were more intelligent or harder working than their counterparts in other parts of the world. Chinese scientists had invented useful things like gunpowder and writing paper centuries before they were known about in the West. The Arabs invented the decimal system. However, other civilizations did not persist and excel in science like the Europeans. From England and the continent of Europe, modern science emerged as an unprecedented, historically powerful force for productivity and the creation of wealth.

The printing press with moveable metal type was invented by Johannes Gutenberg in Germany in 1436. The Bible was the first substantial publication Gutenberg printed in 1455. Since that day until now, the Bible has been the most published and printed book throughout the world. Eventually, the Catholic Church opposed and even suppressed scientific advancement. However, God gave Europe the Reformation that brought the Bible back as the primary foundation of Christian faith. As a result of the Reformation, the Bible was translated into many of the languages of the common people. The Reformers did much to restore the Bible as the standard, not only for religion, but also for all aspects of life. In those days, many Western scientists were strong believers. Isaac Newton (1642-1727), an English mathematician and physicist, was one of the foremost scientists of all time. He formulated a scientific method that was universal in scope, and it still provides a foundation for the way scientists think today. Although his approach was purely logical, Newton believed deeply in the sovereignty of God over all of nature. He believed that the beauty and symmetry of the natural world could only "proceed from the counsel and dominion of an intelligent and powerful Being."

Blaise Pascal (1623-1662) was a French mathematician and an outstanding Christian. He is known for developing the first mechanical computer (the modern computer language PASCAL is named after him). Michael Faraday (1791-1867), who discovered the induction of electric current, was another scientific pioneer with strong biblical faith. These Christian scientists and others like them were a part of the great turning point in history that began in England during the 1700s, called the Industrial Revolution. It changed Europe from a primarily agricultural society to one based on manufacturing, and it provided the foundation for our own modern technological civilization. From Europe came inventions like the steam engine, the internal combustion engine, the jet engine, antibiotics, and the X-ray, as well as guided missiles and dynamite. Scientific advancement and the resulting industrial changes made Europe wealthy as well as politically and militarily powerful. Was this because the Europeans were more brilliant than other people groups on the planet? Did they work harder? No, it is because the Holy Spirit directed Paul's journey west, and Europeans became the recipients of the Bible's message. They received revelation of the Creator God, and they understood the powerful truths of His creation.

The American Age

Eventually, the success of Christianity in Europe became its own limiting factor. By the 1600s, the institutionalized Church was becoming too strong and was wielding too much political power. Dissent was stifled and new movements of the Holy Spirit were persecuted. Believers like the Puritans, Quakers, Mennonites, Huguenots, and early Baptists searched for a place where they would be free to worship God and practice their religion according to their understanding of the Bible. Where could believers go if they were forced to leave the continent of now civilized Europe? Moving further westward, the gospel eventually overflowed the banks of the Old World and came to the New World of the American frontier. The earliest European settlers in North America were mostly pilgrims seeking religious freedom. America was a harsh and undeveloped land. It took great commitment and sacrifice to settle there. Many of these pilgrim pioneers died of disease or starvation during the journey across the Atlantic Ocean, or in the first years of their settlement in the New World.

In their fascinating book, *The Light and the Glory*, authors Peter Marshall and David Manuel chronicle the history of the United States in light of God's divine plan. In their research, they uncovered journals written by Christopher Columbus in which he wrote about his conviction that "the Almighty had singled out him, of all the men of his age, for the honor of bearing the light of Christ to a new world!" According to Marshall and Manuel, the Puritans who came later from England were filled with a sense of godly destiny, and they believed they had a mandate to build a "new Jerusalem" or a model of God's kingdom in North America. It was the vision, faith, and courage of the early Puritan pilgrims that made it possible for the United States to be established as a nation with Christian roots. The Puritans believed they were a covenant people in line with the covenants God had made with Abraham and the people of Israel. They based their new communities on covenants with God. Marshall and Manuel wrote:

And as each church-community grew and became, in effect, a town, these covenants provided the pattern for the first successful civil governments in the western hemisphere. Historians and sociologists alike have long regarded the early New England town meetings as the purest and most successful form that democracy has ever taken. But few, if any, have acknowledged what lay at the core of how and why they worked so well. There would be many modifications, but American democracy owes its inception to the covenants of the first churches on her shores.

As a consequence of the sinful nature of the human race, the history of civilization is filled with periods of brutality and oppression. The history of the Church is not complete without mentioning that it too was marred by dark seasons of injustice and outright sin. The Crusades and the Spanish Inquisition are only two of the better-known examples. It is also true that European colonists and their descendants oppressed the native peoples of America and other parts of the world. Without condoning the sins of these European forefathers, we can say that it was God's plan to bring the gospel to America from Europe and for biblical beliefs to become foundational for American society.

The early pilgrims persisted, and their colonies grew. The colonists insisted on including religious freedom in the laws written for the towns and the new society they were establishing. When the time came for the colonies to break away politically from England, a Declaration of Independence was written, appealing to God's sovereignty as the basis for the rightful demand of liberty. Among the first words of this declaration are, "We hold these truths to be self-evident, that all men are created equal, that they are endowed by their Creator with certain unalienable rights, that among these are life, liberty and the pursuit of happiness." Later, the United States Constitution was drafted on a foundation strongly influenced by the Bible that further protected American freedoms. The First Amendment to the Constitution specifically ensured the freedom of worship. It states, "Congress shall make no law respecting an establishment of religion, or prohibiting the free exercise thereof;" these freedoms, especially the freedom to worship God without government interference, helped propel a fledgling nation to superpower status in less than three hundred years.

French nobleman, Alexis de Tocqueville (1805-1859) visited the United States in 1831, at the height of the Second Great Awakening. This was the time when revivals were sweeping the country, bringing reform to the established cities and primitive frontier areas. In his social and political study of the United States, entitled *Democracy in America*, Tocqueville wrote, "the religious atmosphere of the country was the first thing that struck me on arrival in the United States."

In a relatively short time, the United States became the wealthiest and most powerful nation on Earth. By the end of the twentieth century, American military power had fought against German expansionism in World War I, Nazism, and Fascism during World War II, and then protected Europe from Communism in the Cold War. American science forged ahead using the foundations laid by European predecessors. Inventiveness marked America's rise as a technological world power. Scientific inventions produced by Americans include the electric light bulb, the phonograph, telegraph and the telephone, the airplane, the personal computer and the Internet, radio, television, radar, sonar, fiber optics, satellite communications, stealth aircraft, and the cruise missile. Americans were among the pioneers of genetic science and nuclear energy (and weapons) development.

When I was a child, our family lived near Washington D. C., and I remember pledging allegiance to the American flag each morning in our classrooms. Schoolchildren are no longer required to recite this pledge, but I still remember the words. The United States has been a godly example of "one nation under God … with liberty and justice for all" for countless millions. Christian faith of all varieties flourished in America, and the United States continues to be a great national force for the spreading of the gospel throughout the world. The modern missionary movement began in England with William Carey, but the United States has sent out more people and other mission resources than any other nation to the rest of the world.

Today, however, America desperately needs a fresh touch from God. The steady decline in church attendance, popular entertainment that exalts the sadistic and immoral, and mass killings perpetrated by school children are among the signs of deep spiritual crisis. The foundations are being eroded. No society can grow much beyond its ethical and moral base or its collective vision of the world. A powerful national vision must, first of all, be based on morality and truth. This is essential for the establishment of genuine social justice and hope for the future. To have these absolutes, a nation's mind must be anchored in the existence of the Creator God, the ultimate judge of good and evil, who dwells beyond our human limitations. Christian thinker, Francis Schaeffer said it well when he wrote, "The problem is not outward things. The problem is having, and then acting upon, the right worldview—the worldview which gives men and women the truth of what is." Today, recognizing the growing spiritual peril, many well-known Christian leaders have joined the chorus of urgent cries for national repentance and spiritual renewal in America.

Even though the Church in America still may appear strong in many ways, especially when viewed from the outside, there is an ongoing, steady retreat of the gospel as a sanctifying influence in American culture. The myth of the "moral majority" has been shattered, and spiritually reborn Christians realize now that they are effectively a minority and their tactics must change accordingly. The popular culture and the media can no longer be considered neutral. In general, they are forces opposed to the biblical worldview and lifestyle. However, when believers in America choose their targets carefully and focus efforts in either prayer or political activism, victories can be won.

The Wave Continues

While the Church in America labors to strengthen things that remain and cries out for revival, the crest of the wave of new gospel expansion is continuing to move westward. Leaping the great Pacific Ocean, it is crashing on the shores of the Far East, changing forever the cultural and spiritual coastlines of nations like Korea, China, Singapore, and the Philippines. In Asian nations, the gospel of Jesus is powerfully impacting Buddhist, Confucian, Hindu, and animistic cultures. The tsunami of Christian faith has come to Asia in this generation. In the past, God showed favor and gave His glory to Europe and North America. They were raised to incredible heights of honor, power, and wealth. Although pagan in their beginnings, these nations chose to serve Him and advance His purposes in the world. The God of the Bible does not show partiality, and He will release His power to any nation that allows the gospel to penetrate to the roots of culture.

Today, missions strategists tell us the bulk of the remaining unreached peoples live in what has been termed the *10/40 Window*. This is a narrow strip of the globe between the latitudes of 10 and 40 degrees north and bounded by Korea on the east and North Africa on the west. If North Africa is included in the Islamic world (which has its demographic and religious center of gravity somewhere between Djakarta and Mecca), Israel is found at the westernmost reach of the 10/40 Window. Israel, where it all started, is the end of the line in the western sweep of world evangelization.

Jerusalem is God's chosen place for the return of the Messiah, and the chosen time is also described in Scripture. Israel's revival will follow the fullness of God's harvest among all nations. (See Romans 11:25-26.) The completion of this harvest is the chief requirement that Jesus personally gave for His return. When asked directly by His disciples about the signs of His return, He said, *"And this gospel of the kingdom shall be preached in the whole world for a witness to all the nations, and*

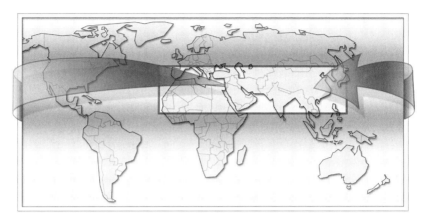

Rectangle represents the "10/40 Window" of unreached nations.

then the end shall come" (Matthew 24:14). In biblical Greek, the word *witness* is from the same root word as *martyr*. The meaning of being a witness is not limited to being killed, but it also means to give up your life for the Lord in smaller but meaningful ways. Preaching the gospel as a witness, therefore, is more than short wave radio or satellite television broadcasts. It means that there will be a viable church community *on the ground* in that nation with indigenous believers serving and laying down their lives daily in the midst of their own culture. It means that there will be houses of worship built and the Word of God spoken in the native languages. It means there will be a public move of God's Spirit bringing men and women into the Kingdom of God.

Europe has had the gospel for almost twenty centuries. America has received several great spiritual awakenings in the last three hundred years of its history. The names of great Christian leaders are associated with these successive North American waves of the gospel. Men like Jonathan Edwards and George Whitefield, Charles G. Finney, D. L. Moody, Billy Graham, and Bill Bright rode the waves of God's grace as it visited America. I, myself, am the product of one of these waves, the "Jesus Movement," which swept across the United States from the west coast in the 1960s. At the same time, there are nations like Iran and Saudi Arabia that have never had even one great move of God's Holy Spirit. Before He returns, the Sovereign Lord will demonstrate His love and the goodness of His gospel in all the nations of the world.

The ramifications of this geographic understanding of the gospel's expansion are profound. Similar to the laborers hired late in the day described in Jesus' parable of Matthew, chapter 20, first-generation Christians in Asia are receiving the rich rewards of the Kingdom (and the benefit of centuries-old Western Christian tradition). There is a significant difference between those cultures that are in front of God's worldwide revival wave, those riding the wave, and those behind the wave. In front of the wave, the work of ministry is characterized by preparation. As in the case of Israel, the significance of God's work is prophetic and future-oriented. For those nations on the crest of the wave, it is a time of great harvest and church growth. For those nations behind the wave, there can be revival based on an existing spiritual legacy and the recovery of sound spiritual foundations. God's overall purpose is the evangelization of the world, but His strategy varies for each nation depending on their position relative to His tidal wave of revival.

Tsunami in Latin America and Africa

God's tsunami of revival has been sweeping Latin America in recent years. Churches have been growing for several decades, and now revival leaders like Carlos Annacondia and Cesar Castellanos are launching out internationally to touch other nations. The testimony of revival in South and Central America is having an impact around the world. Recently, while ministering in Switzerland, I was invited to an evening service at a church in Lausanne. I encountered an on fire congregation, worshipping the Lord with all their heart and strength in

Spanish. They were among the thousands of guest workers from South and Central America working in that city. I told them that their nations, former colonies of European powers, have a mandate to re-evangelize Europe for the Lord's glory.

In Africa, waves of revival have been passing through for a generation or more. Multitudes have been converted to Christianity, but they have not been discipled. Many Africans accepted Christian terminology and outward symbols, but often the gospel has not seeped down deeply enough into the roots of African culture and tribal society. In the 1960s, Africa was called the most "Christianized" continent. Even today, the world's largest public Christian gatherings take place in Africa. However recently, bloody conflicts between rival "Christian" tribes have exposed faith that may be real, but certainly shallow. It has been said by some that, "Christianity in Africa is a mile wide, and an inch deep." Ministries that confront the priority of tribal identity with the culture of God's kingdom, and churches that will teach and disciple rather than simply evangelize, are sorely needed in Africa.

At the same time, God's incredible grace is continually being poured out on Africa today. One of our young leaders from Mount Carmel spent a year working with orphans in Mozambique, one of the poorest countries in the world. There he worked alongside humble pastors who not only preached the gospel and healed the sick, but also raised several people from the dead by prayer. Other documented reports of significant miracles have come out of Africa in recent days, and African Christians are increasingly reaching out to other nations. I have been told that the largest church in Europe is a congregation of more than twenty thousand in Kiev, Ukraine. The founding pastor there is a Russian-speaking Nigerian who was once recruited by the Communists, but is now serving the King of kings.

The expansion of God's kingdom in Europe has much to do with the growing church in Africa. Today, there are more

Anglicans in Nigeria than in England. Moreover, the African Anglicans are holding to a more literal view of the Scriptures, and their churches are growing while in England and the United States Anglicans and Episcopalians are moving away from the clear moral teaching of the Bible and some of their strongest congregations are leaving the communion. Recently, while teaching at a pastors' conference in Geneva, I was delighted to meet many vibrant French-speaking Christians from a variety of African nations. Their children are all French-born and serving God with vigor.

For young believers launching out in ministry and looking for a place to invest their lives, I will use the example of surfing. I don't mean surfing the Internet, but the old-fashioned surfing in the ocean with a surfboard. The *prophetic* secret of surfing is to catch the wave of God's purposes as it sweeps through your generation. Catching it requires correct positioning and recognizing the chosen moment. You wait with your board correctly positioned out in front of the approaching waves. This is the prophetic part, which takes wisdom and discernment. You must know where the wave is coming from and where it is going. You must get to a place of personal discipline and freedom, out in front of it. Then you wait upon the Lord. There are waves, and then there is *The Big Wave*. When you see The Big Wave coming, you must paddle to gain momentum, but it is not about your effort. It is all about catching the power that is in God's wave. You paddle in the right direction so that the wave catches you. God's power and purposes will take you for the ride of your life!

Everyone knows that the real action and the excitement of surfing takes place at the edge of the wave. When you see first-generation Christians coming to the Lord all around you and people with no previous New Testament heritage filling churches by the thousands, you are looking at the edge of the wave. Centuries ago, God's tsunami swept across Europe. Three hundred years ago, it began to flow mightily into

America. Especially in the last one hundred and fifty years, Africa and South America have felt the impact of this great wave. Now God's tsunami is moving faster, and it is many times larger than ever before. Today, this massive wave of the gospel is sweeping across Asia from the east toward the west.

Tsunami in Asia

God's tsunami is cresting in China, Korea, and other parts of East Asia. To the west, India is only beginning to move into an era of historic church growth and even further west; the Islamic countries of Central Asia are starting to sense a spiritual stirring. The Islamic world as a whole is beginning to feel the impact of this spiritual wave. Militant Islam, such as is found today in Iran, regards the West (America and Europe) as the "Great Satan." Islam's greatest military and political threat is in fact coming from the west, but it is the gospel coming from Islam's east that will ultimately transform this giant through intercessory prayer and evangelism. Korean missionaries are going forth into Central Asia in greater numbers each year. It is said that today's revival in South Korea actually began in the north, sparked by the great Welsh revival many years before the Korean War divided the country. In those days the rallying cry of the church was, "Pyongyang to Jerusalem!" There was a vision to bring the gospel to all of Asia, including the land of the Bible. That vision is becoming reality today.

Economic hardship in the Philippines has resulted in millions of Filipinos living and working in foreign countries as Overseas Filipino Workers (OFWs). Most OFWs are known to their employers as soft-spoken, polite, English-speaking, diligent workers. They are highly prized throughout the world as caregivers for the elderly and infirm, and as nannies or domestics. Several million Filipinos work in Central Asia and the Middle East. Tens of thousands of them are born-again Christians. If these Christians were to be considered missionaries, it would be the largest mission force ever sent out by a single nation in history. Increasingly, they are being trained and mobilized as intercessors and teachers. In extremely closed countries like Saudi Arabia (where there are 1.5 million OFWs), there have been reports of Filipino Christians who were executed by Islamic authorities for conducting secret worship meetings. Truly, they are martyrs for the Lord.

The Church in Singapore has received a revelation that their nation is called by God to be the "Antioch of Asia." In New Testament times, the city of Antioch was a beehive of church activities and the launching place for the Apostle Paul and other trans-local ministries. Singapore is a city-state of only three and one-half million people. Although small in size, it has emerged as a regional economic leader through the astute leadership of its founder and former senior minister, Lee Kuan Yew. The country is governed by ranks of very professional civil servants and has been rated one of the least corrupt nations in the world. Freedom of religion is protected as long as certain social balances are respected. As a result, the Church in Singapore has grown not only in size, but also in maturity and awareness of their unique prophetic calling. Singaporean Christians are pioneering creative ways to bring the gospel to many neighboring countries in South East Asia.

Rapid Church growth among the ethnic Chinese has impacted all of South East Asia, especially countries like Malaysia and Indonesia. These two nations are on the front line where the tsunami of Asian Christian growth meets the Islamic world. We can expect significant changes in these societies during the near future. Large churches have grown up among the ethnic Chinese, but the expansion of Christianity into the wider population has been hampered by Islamic resistance, government opposition to evangelism, and ethnic differences. In Thailand, however, the ethnic Chinese are well integrated into the general population, mixing easily with indigenous Thai people and other tribal groups. As Church growth gains momentum in Thailand, it may not encounter the barriers found in some of it neighboring countries. Despite government persecution, the Church in countries like Vietnam, Laos, and Myanmar is growing.

Japan today is in a spiritual crisis. The government's official figures on suicide show that there have been more than 30,000 suicides each year for more than a decade. Most people believe the government figures reflect only the reported suicides and that many families are hesitant to report a suicide because of the shame involved. The grim statistics reveal that not only young people are dying but also the number of suicides by middle-aged men has risen dramatically. These men are the "salary men": the generation of working people who carried the burden of the Japanese economic *miracle* through hard work and devotion to their companies. Today's crisis in Japan is not, in essence, an economic crisis, but rather a crisis of vision. Japanese people have not stopped working hard nor have they lost their ability to produce quality goods and services. Instead, they have lost confidence in their nation's leadership and the social compass used to guide their country into the future. Much of Japan's modern history can be summed up by the motto, "Catch up with the West!" Today, having the world's second largest national economy, Japan has not only caught up, but has surpassed most of the Western world, at least in terms of worldly wealth. However, catching up is one thing and leading is another. In order to lead, there must be a powerful vision given to a nation by the living God. That vision must have deep concern for the welfare of all peoples as an integral part. Japan today is in a crisis of sacrificing an old national vision in order to grasp the new.

In the last century, Japan has twice tried to become a powerful world leader. The first attempt was the militarist expansion that began before the Second World War. This ended in military defeat for Japan and the disastrous atomic attacks on Hiroshima and Nagasaki. Japan's second attempt at world leadership was through post-war industrial and commercial expansion. This chapter came to a close in the 1990s with the bursting of the economic bubble and more than a decade of low or negative economic growth. However, the day is coming when God will allow Japan to become an influence in the world through the gospel.

Over one hundred years ago, Japanese Christian leader Uchimura Kanzo wrote, "As no man lives for himself alone, so no nation exists for itself alone. The destiny of Japan is intimately connected with that of one billion Asiatics and they are to be blessed or cursed as we behave truly or falsely." The population figure in Asia is now closer to three billion. However, the destiny of Japan as seen by Uchimura has not been revoked. Japan's calling is still to be a blessing to the people of Asia. Many Japanese Christians might say, "We are small in number and lacking financial and political power. Since we are not a real force in our own nation, how can we bless the other nations?" It was not long ago, in a bombed-out Japan threatened with starvation, that men like Sony's Ibuka and Morita began dreaming of a successful electronics business. Postwar Japan, coming out of the ashes of war's devastation, produced men like Honda and Matsushita, giants who built corporations that have influenced the entire world. There are men and women of great spiritual potential hidden in the Japanese Church today. It is time for them to speak out with God's vision, not just to the Christians in the churches, but also to the entire nation.

Australia is a country on the Asian side of the Pacific with a unique European heritage. Established as a British penal colony in 1788, Australia has grown into a prosperous nation with a strong industrial base. Church attendance is shrinking, and the country is facing a spiritual identity crisis. Will Australia successfully break with its European parentage and join the spiritual dynamic of the Asian tsunami to the north? Australia has a strategic position in Asia as a base for training workers and supporting the massive movement of the gospel in its closest neighbor, Indonesia (the world's most populous Islamic nation) and throughout the region. God will bless Australia with revival as it spiritually joins with Asia in creating a new regional Christian identity that spans racial and cultural differences.

Back to Jerusalem

We live in a time when it is possible to envision the events leading up to the completion of Jesus' Great Commission. One day in the not so distant future, the Chinese government policy against believers in Jesus will be changed. The massive underground network of house churches will surface, and the unbelieving world, along with many Christians all over the world, will be stunned by their sheer numbers and the strength of their faith. God has invested so much over the years in the Chinese church. Many martyrs, both Western and Chinese, have shed their blood on Chinese soil, and now tens of millions pursue lives of faith in defiance of official (and unofficial) government persecution. Today, China, in spite of its great size, is also one of the world's fastest growing economies. One day it may be the world's largest. God's hand is behind this, and His purposes are being fulfilled in China. This nation will lead the Christian world in taking action to complete God's work of bringing in the "fullness of the Gentiles."

Brother Yun, a leader in the huge network of Chinese believers called the Sinim Fellowship, has written a truly stirring book documenting his miraculous survival under imprisonment and torture. He portrays the vision and struggle of the house-church movement in China in striking terms. In the book, *The Heavenly Man*, written with Paul Hattaway, Brother Yun tells of the Chinese "Back to Jerusalem" Movement that began with a small band of believers in Shandong Province in the 1920s. Their goal was to preach the gospel to all the lands between China and Jerusalem. Today, the "Back to Jerusalem" Movement is alive and growing in China. Brother Yun wrote:

You need to understand that when we speak about "Back to Jerusalem" we're not saying that Jerusalem is the main goal. We are not planning to rush there for a big conference! Jerusalem was the starting point for the gospel two thousand years ago and we believe it will circle the whole world and return to its starting point. Our aim is not merely to evangelize the city of Jerusalem, but the thousands of unreached people, groups, towns, and villages located between China and Jerusalem. The vision for Back to Jerusalem is now the primary goal of all the house church leaders in the Sinim Fellowship. This is not one project we have among many. This is the main thrust and focus of all our activities. We talk about it over breakfast, lunch, and dinner. We pray unceasingly, asking God to raise up labourers and remove all obstacles. We dream about it in our sleep.

Israel's Hope: The Gospel From the East

Israel, the place where the gospel message originated, is at the very western edge of the Asian continent. Scripture predicts that the site of Messiah's return will be on the Mount of Olives in the city of Jerusalem. How and when will the great tsunami of revival come to the land of the Bible? Israel, the first nation to receive the gospel, must now wait for the other nations to have their chance. The Apostle Paul wrote, *"… that blindness in part has happened to Israel until the fullness of the Gentiles has come in"* (Romans 11:25). Jesus himself said, *"And Jerusalem will be trampled by Gentiles until the times of the Gentiles are fulfilled"* (Luke 21:24b). When the work of the Kingdom is fully completed in all of Asia, Christians from the east of Israel (including Arab former Muslims) will play a key role in bringing the gospel message to Israel. Just as the kings came from the east to herald the birth of the Messiah in Israel, Christians from Central Asia and the Arab world will come to Jerusalem saying,

The sealed Eastern Gate of Jerusalem's old city.

"The time of the Gentiles is fulfilled. Prepare for the return of the Messiah!" This will complete the global circumnavigation of the gospel. End-time spiritual revival in Israel will fulfill Jesus' prophecy, *"Thus the last shall be first, and the first last"* (Matthew 20:16).

Traditionally, Israel's Messiah is believed to be coming from the east. The tabernacle that Moses built in the wilderness was always positioned with its main entrance facing toward the rising of the sun. Solomon's temple in Jerusalem and Herod's temple both faced the east. It is through the Golden Gate (also called the Beautiful Gate or the Eastern Gate) in the eastern wall of Old Jerusalem, that the Messiah is expected to enter the city. This was the most important of Jerusalem's gates in Jesus' time since it was the city entrance that faced the front of the Great Temple. Later, Christians declared that Jesus would return to Jerusalem through this gate. As a result, it was sealed by the

Muslim leader Saladin in 1187, and remains closed to this day. Ezekiel's prophecy contains a vision of God's glory filling His temple. Ezekiel wrote, *"Then he led me to the gate, the gate facing toward the east; and behold the glory of the God of Israel was coming from the way of the east ... And the glory of the Lord came into the house by way of the gate facing toward the east"* (Ezekiel 43:1-2a; 4, NASB).

The End-time Clock

It has been said that Israel is "God's end-time clock," and that the hands of the clock are approaching twelve midnight, indicating the soon return of the Lord. By understanding God's actions toward Israel, many believe that the timetable of the Messiah's return can be gauged. I agree that Israel is an important key to developing an eschatology that is in sync with the world of history and current affairs. However, there are two hands on the end-time clock. Israel is the short hand—the hour hand of the clock—and it is approaching midnight and the return of the Lord. However, the long hand of the clock is the hand of the nations. The term "nations" is first found in the Bible in Genesis, chapter 10. After the flood and Noah's deliverance through the ark, God divided the people of the world into nations. This division was part of His plan to redeem creation. In Matthew, chapter 24, Jesus said that all nations must receive the gospel as a witness before His return. The long hand of the end-time clock that represents the nations has a few more revolutions to go before we can say that the prophetic Scriptures are fulfilled and the world is ready for the Messiah's return.

Consider the following scenario as if you are an evangelist or church planter in western China today. You have seen several hundred thousand first-generation Christians come to the Lord through your ministry and the work of your team over the last ten or fifteen years. However, to the west of you are regions that have yet to hear the gospel. Many people in these other areas have never heard the gospel even once. In fact, none of their ancestors as far back as anyone can remember has ever responded to the gospel. You know that given more time, more resources, and more workers, you could personally help perhaps a million more people come into the Kingdom of God during your lifetime. If you were this Chinese evangelist, what would you be requesting from the Lord in prayer? You would not be crying out for His hasty return. You would be asking Him to wait and to thrust out more laborers and other resources into the harvest.

If you were the Lord of the Harvest, what would you do? Europe has had the gospel for about nineteen centuries. The United States has had the gospel for three hundred years, enough time for several great spiritual awakenings to ripple through the population. Africa and South America have also seen revival within the last century, but Asia is only beginning its revival now. If you were the Lord, would you cut off the evangelization of the world before the work is finished? The Islamic world has never seen a widespread awakening of New Testament faith. Short-term eschatologies that truncate God's stated objectives for the spread of the gospel throughout the world deny the justice of God and have a limited view of His strategic plan for the nations.

There is a difference between preaching the imminent return of the Lord and the immediate return. The imminent return means that Jesus could come at any time like "a thief in the night." We need to be ready to meet Him, even if the time is this afternoon or tonight. Spiritual preparedness is part of the discipline of a true disciple. At the same time, we know that a thousand years is "as a day to the Lord" and that there is also a good chance He will not return in our lifetimes. Since the Church was born almost two thousand years ago, every generation of Christians has had those who believed Jesus would return while they were alive. All those who believed that theirs would be the last generation have been wrong until the present day. Disciples of Jesus need to wait upon the Lord with patience and endurance, with our "lamps lit" like the five wise virgins in Matthew, chapter 25, even if He appears to delay.

Today we are in the midst of the greatest revival of Christian faith since the Day of Pentecost. More people are becoming believers and are being baptized than ever before in history. It is no accident that these days of great revival should coincide with the restoration of Israel and the resurrection of the remnant of Messianic Jewish believers. These are prophetic signs of the end-times, and even greater events will be revealed as we progress further in time. The unfolding mystery of Israel's resurrection as a nation is an important key to understanding the events leading up to the Lord's return and the culmination of human history.

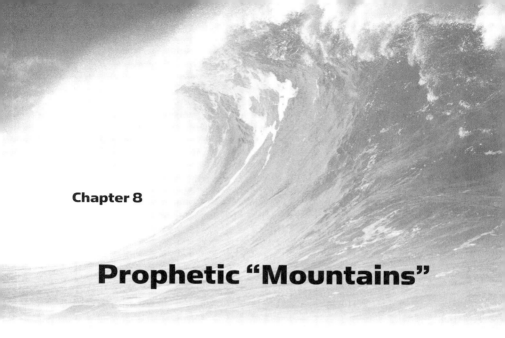

Chapter 8

Prophetic "Mountains"

PROPHETIC EVENTS CAN BE LIKE MOUNTAINS. If you catch the revelation of a great prophetic event and pursue it, the result can be like climbing a spiritual mountain. You may have to struggle to find the trail and stay on it, but at the top, you can see far more than at the bottom. Your vision is extended, your horizon stretched. However, sometimes it is hard to recognize the true significance of these prophetic events when they are *close up*—happening in our own times.

If someone were to bring you blindfolded to the base of Mount Everest, remove the blindfold, and ask you to describe what you saw, probably you would say, "I see a pile of rocks!" It is only by moving away from the mountain that you would begin to appreciate its size. Stepping back you might then say, "That's a *big* pile of rocks." Further back you would remark, "That's not just a big pile of rocks, but a mountain." Even further away you might realize, "That's not just a mountain, but a giant mountain!"

One such mountain of revelation was the coming of Jesus the Messiah. His incarnation and redeeming ministry tower as a huge mountain of fulfilled prophecy over other events of history. John, one of the eyewitnesses who climbed the mountain of Jesus' revelation, wrote, *"That which was from the beginning, which we have heard, which we have seen with our eyes, which we have looked upon, and our hands have handled, concerning the Word of life. ... "* (1 John 1:1). The disciples of Jesus were overwhelmed with a sense of awe about what had been revealed to them—and rightly so. Only one other event will be greater than what they experienced, and that will be the Lord's return.

Let us examine these two prophetic mountains of Jesus' incarnation and return. If we line them up and look at them so that one is in front of the other, it may appear that the return of Jesus will occur immediately after His first coming. Indeed, many generations of Christians believed that He would return in their own time. However, when these mountains are viewed from any other angle, it is clear that there is a long valley in between them. Today, we know that valley is at least two thousand years long. It is the valley of the gospel going out among all the nations, and it is the valley of Israel's dispersion. If we look more closely, we find there are other mountains between these two large ones that we couldn't see previously. These other mountains were blocked from view by the first massive mountain of the Messiah's incarnation. One of these mountains could be the Reformation, and another, the Pentecostal movement. However, one of the largest mountains in the valley is the mountain of Israel's return to the land of promise and its resurrection as a modern nation.

Once we ascend this mountain of Israel's modern restoration and have a revelatory understanding of its significance, we can see more clearly into the spiritual landscape that remains until we will arrive at the huge event of Jesus the Messiah's return. Climbing the mountain of Israel's prophetic significance helps identify the sequence of major events that lead to the return of the Lord.

Prophecy: Moral and Purposeful

When it comes to understanding prophecy, it is crucially important to get the timing right. We may be completely correct about what God will do, but miss the timing. This can cause confusion and spiritual damage. The test of biblical prophecy is when God's Word in Scripture intersects with His actions in history. There are some basic principles for understanding the dynamic of God's prophetic word. The first is that God's Word is eternal. What God says always reflects His unchanging holy character and everlasting love. In the Bible, God commits himself to faithfully honoring His Word. The Psalmist wrote, *"You have magnified Your word above all Your name"* (Psalm 138:2). Isaiah, the prophet said, *"The grass withers, the flower fades, but the word of our God stands forever"* (Isaiah 40:8). Jesus, the perfect image of the Father, is called the Word of God. The great Christmas hymn, "O Come, All Ye Faithful," contains these lyrics, based on the first chapter of John's gospel, "Word of the Father, now in flesh appearing, O come, let us adore Him."

Secondly, because God is holy and pure, His prophetic word is moral. Biblical prophets denounced sin and accurately predicted its judgment. They prophesied the lifting up of the righteous and the vindication of God's faithful servants. If we as students of prophecy and God's disciples understand His morality, we will understand God's actions toward us and our world. If we live in holiness like priests, separated to the service of the Holy One, we can participate in the manifestation of God's prophetic word to our generation. If we love holiness and live by faith according to a holy standard, God will counsel with us. He will deliver His prophetic word to a sinful world through sanctified vessels. God's morality reveals to us God's character, and tells us what He will do.

However, morality alone does not tell us everything we need to know about prophecy. Ultimately, God's actions are purposeful. He has a plan to accomplish in every life and in the creation as a whole. Morality may tell us what God will do, but understanding God's purposes will tell us when and how He will do it. Certainly, God will judge sin, but when and how? Why does God sometimes seem to wait so long, and why do His judgments sometimes come without delay? Why are God's judgments sometimes direct and fast, like laser-guided missiles, and sometimes difficult to see? Is it possible to predict how God will correct a grievous and sinful situation, either by immediate, forceful intervention or by patient persuasion? When should we prophesy judgment, and when is God showing mercy? Prophetic wisdom on our part requires understanding God's character as well as respecting His sovereign purposes as He works out His plans in our world.

Lazarus' Death and Resurrection

Read carefully the following story from John's gospel. Contained in it is an analogy that relates God's heart toward Israel to Jesus' behavior with His friends.

> *Now a certain man was sick, Lazarus of Bethany, the town of Mary and her sister Martha. It was that Mary who anointed the Lord with fragrant oil and wiped His feet with her hair, whose brother Lazarus was sick. Therefore the sisters sent to Him, saying, "Lord, behold, he whom You love is sick." When Jesus heard that, He said, "**This sickness is not unto death, but for the glory of God, that the Son of God may be glorified through it.**" Now Jesus loved Martha and her sister and Lazarus. So, when He heard that he was sick, He stayed two more days in the place where He was. Then after this He said to the disciples, "Let us go to Judea again"* (John 11:1-7).

Mary, Martha, and their brother Lazarus lived in Bethany, near Jerusalem. They were personal friends of the Lord, and He loved them. Although Jesus was in Galilee with His disciples, the sisters sent for Him when Lazarus became ill. When the messenger arrived, the Lord said, "This sickness is not unto death...." He then stayed two more days in the north of the country before finally heading south to Judea and the Jerusalem area. The messenger must have preceded Him, going back to the home of Mary and Martha with the good news, "The Lord says your brother is not going to die but that God is going to be glorified!" On the way, Jesus told His disciples that Lazarus was "asleep," and that they were going to wake him up. Puzzled, the disciples questioned Him about this. Finally, Jesus told them clearly, *"Lazarus is dead. And I am glad for your sakes that I was not there, that you may believe. Nevertheless let us go to him"* (John 11:14-15). John records that when they arrived in Bethany, Lazarus had been in the grave for four days.

It is Jewish tradition to bury the deceased as quickly as possible after death. In Judaism, dead bodies are ritually unclean. Even today, funerals can take place the same day as the death, and they are rarely more than one or two days later. Jewish funerals are very stark. No coffin or casket is used, and cremation is not considered a part of Jewish tradition. The body of the departed person is simply wrapped in white cloth and transported to the burial plot amid the crying and mourning of the family and friends. Little is done to diminish the fact that the body is being returned to the earth from which it was formed. After the funeral, it is traditional for the family to wear clothes that have been purposefully torn, and then they sit in their house for seven days. This is called "sitting shiva" and is taken from the Hebrew word *sheva*, meaning the number seven. While a family sits shiva, friends and relatives visit and sit with them. Typically, visitors will bring some food and will keep the mourners company, crying together while looking at pictures of the deceased, and remembering good times shared while he or she was alive.

When Jesus arrived in Bethany, Mary and Martha were sitting shiva. Their house had visitors, some of whom had probably shared the last hours of Lazarus' life with him, praying, and hoping for his recovery. It was a very sad day. John does not record whether Mary and Martha's father was still alive. Perhaps Lazarus was the only adult male in the family, the only breadwinner. In spite of their sorrow, when word reached the sisters of Jesus' approach, both Martha and Mary went out individually to greet the Master.

According to John's account, both sisters said exactly the same thing to Him, "Lord, if You had been here, my brother would not have died." (See John 11:21 and 32.) Can we hear their true emotions in these words? What they said was not just a declaration of faith in their famous friend. Weren't they also saying "Where were you, Jesus? Why didn't you come to save Lazarus? Didn't you send word he was not going to die? We thought our brother was your friend. Why didn't you come to heal him?" Mary and Martha had been through the soul-wrenching process of watching their brother weaken and die, all the while holding onto the hope that he would live according to the words they had received by the messenger. Lazarus himself must have held onto that hope until he was too weak to continue. The horror of separation had come upon them along with the realization that the Master had apparently been wrong this time—when it really counted, in a life or death situation. The family had been through much pain by the time Jesus arrived. It is understandable that despair, bitterness, or even reproach was behind their simple words. No wonder, Jesus groaned within His spirit and wept at their lack of faith as He approached the tomb of his friend.

*Then they took away the stone from the place where the dead man was lying. And Jesus lifted up His eyes and said, "Father, I thank You that You have heard Me. And I know that You always hear Me, **but because*** *of the people who are standing by I said this, that they may believe that You sent Me."* Now when He had said these things, He cried with a loud voice, "Lazarus, come forth!" And he who had died came out bound hand and foot with graveclothes, and his face was wrapped with a cloth. Jesus said to them, "Loose him, and let him go." *Then many of the Jews who had come to Mary, and had seen the things Jesus did, believed in Him* (John 11:41-45).

God's purpose in raising Lazarus from the grave was not simply to make Lazarus live for a few more years. If that were so, Jesus could have arranged to have arrived in Bethany earlier and prevented his death. The morality of God does not explain why He deliberately allowed Lazarus, a beloved friend, to die. In fact, it seems to defy our human understanding of God's mercy that He would require Lazarus and his family to go through the agonies of death and separation just so Jesus could make him alive once more. However, God's redemptive purpose was not limited to Lazarus and his family alone. God's purpose was also for the disciples, for the Jewish nonbelievers in the house, and ultimately, for all believers and readers of the New Testament throughout the centuries.

The greatness of God is that He bears the weight of responsibility for the final outcome of everything in the universe. This eternal responsibility is God's glory. God is light, and He dwells in the light. He is always on display. Every act of God must be an example for the world and for the heavenly host as well as to the dark powers and principalities of Satan. God's choices, therefore, are always suitable as models to lead and teach us. God chose to make Jesus' friend, Lazarus, an example. After Lazarus died and was raised, he was still subject to the normal harshness of life. Later, of course, he died again. However, while he lived, he was a living witness to the power and wisdom of God. What greater friendship could have been shown to him by Jesus than sharing in the same destiny of death and resurrection as the Lord himself? This, for Lazarus, was surely worth the agony of death. The glory that Lazarus shared with Jesus was illustrated when Jesus returned to Bethany months later near the time of Passover.

> *Now a great many of the Jews knew that He was there; and **they came, not for Jesus' sake only, but that they might also see Lazarus**, whom He had raised from the dead. But the chief priests plotted to put Lazarus to death also, because **on account of him many of the Jews went away and believed in Jesus** (John 12:9-11).*

John recorded that unbelieving Jews visited Bethany not only in order to see and hear Jesus, the Master, but also to see his friend Lazarus who had been raised from the dead. Lazarus' testimony was so powerful that the chief priests plotted to kill him. This is actually comical in a dark sort of way. These spiritually blind men may have shelved their assassination plans for fear that Jesus would resurrect him again. What does a man who has already died once have to fear? Because of Lazarus' testimony, many Jews believed in Jesus and were saved by their faith. This was the purpose of God that was finally revealed through the working of His word in the lives of Lazarus and his sisters.

A Prophetic Analogy

The spiritual picture here is that the nation of Israel is like Lazarus. Israel as a nation has been brought back from death after nearly two thousand years of wanderings, persecutions, expulsions, and the Holocaust. The prophet Ezekiel wrote that God showed him a valley of dry bones:

> *Then He said to me, "Son of man, **these bones are the whole house of Israel**. They indeed say, 'Our bones*

are dry, our hope is lost, and we ourselves are cut off!'
Therefore prophesy and say to them, 'Thus says the Lord
GOD: **Behold, O My people, I will open your graves**
and cause you to come up from your graves, and bring
you into the land of Israel.'" (Ezekiel 37:11-12)

This national resurrection is the fulfillment of prophecy for
the Jewish people, but God's purpose is that His glory will be
shown to the other nations so that they might believe. Thousands
of sightseers and pilgrims come to Israel on tour not only to
draw closer to God, but also that they might see Israel, the
nation that is now alive from the dead. When combined with
biblical revelation, the testimony of Israel has the power to
focus the hearts of the nations on the end-time purposes of the
Lord. Israel is God's witness nation that He loves, but Israel has
experienced the agony of death in order to fulfill His purposes.
God's plan since the fall of humankind has been the redemption
of all humans. His glory and His character are shown in His
actions toward Israel, the nation that He selected for a special
role. In looking at some of the prophetic connections between
God's actions toward Israel and His purposes in the nations, a
theme can be seen repeated throughout the Bible.

> *Break forth into joy, sing together, you waste places*
> *of Jerusalem! For the LORD has comforted His people,*
> **he has redeemed Jerusalem.** *The LORD has made bare*
> *His holy arm* **in the eyes of all the nations;** *and all the*
> *ends of the earth shall see the salvation of our God*
> (Isaiah 52:9-10).

> *Then* **they shall dwell in the land that I have given**
> **to Jacob My servant,** *where your fathers dwelt; and they*
> *shall dwell there, they, their children, and their children's*
> *children, forever; and My servant David shall be their*
> *prince forever....* **The nations also will know that I, the**

LORD, sanctify Israel, when My sanctuary is in their midst forevermore (Ezekiel 37:25; 28).

Chapter 9

Israel's Irrevocable Calling

OVER THE YEARS, I have continued to grapple with God's choice of the Jews. It has also been a journey of learning more about God himself. I know Him to be awesome in power and full of unearthly glory, but at the same time, purposeful and efficient in His actions. One of the beauties of God's choices is the function He has designed into them. Each snowflake is different and testifies to the Creator's infinite creativity, and snowflakes falling together serve a necessary function of bringing needed moisture to the Earth. God's choice of Israel is powerful and complex, but also functional. He chose the people of Israel for a deep and far-reaching redemptive purpose.

When God called Abraham to a life of faith, He said:

> *Get out of your country, from your family and from your father's house, to a land that I will show you. I will make you a great nation; I will bless you and make your name great; and you shall be a blessing. I will bless those who bless you, and I will curse him who curses you;*

and in you all the families of the earth shall be blessed (Genesis 12:1-3).

From the start, Abraham's call involved being a blessing to all the nations of the world. God repeated His promise and His purpose after Abraham's faithfulness was tested on the mountain of sacrifice with his son, Isaac. God said, *"In your seed all the nations of the earth shall be blessed, because you have obeyed My voice"* (Genesis 22:18). This clearly was important to the Lord as He repeated the same promise to Abraham's son, Isaac, (See Genesis 26:4.) and to his grandson, Jacob, whom He renamed Israel. God said to Jacob:

> *Also your descendants shall be as the dust of the earth; you shall spread abroad to the west and the east, to the north and the south; and in you and in your seed all the families of the earth shall be blessed* (Genesis 28:14).

It is a fact that Israel as a nation did not accept Jesus as God's promised Messiah. Does the New Testament teach that God rejected His people Israel because they rejected Him? What did Paul, God's messenger to the Church, write?

> *I say then, has God cast away His people? Certainly not! For I also am an Israelite, of the seed of Abraham, of the tribe of Benjamin. God has not cast away His people whom He foreknew ... Even so then, at this present time there is a remnant according to the election of grace* (Romans 11:1-2a; 5).

Even today, most Jewish hearts are not open to the message of salvation through faith in the Messiah. However, God's calling of Israel as a priestly nation will never be revoked. Neither will the spiritual gifts He gave the nation to bless all the peoples of the world. The Apostle Paul wrote, *"… concerning the election they are beloved for the sake of the fathers. For the gifts and the calling of God are irrevocable"* (Romans 11:28b-29).

The Obligation of the Chosen

The door of God's eternal purposes for Israel requires two keys. Later we will see how Jesus passed on those keys for their intended use to His own disciples. One key is the work of local Messianic Jewish congregations. The other equally important key is found among the nations. The great prophet Isaiah described God's fullest intention for Israel and the world when he wrote:

> *Indeed He [the Lord] says, "It is too small a thing that You should be My Servant to raise up the tribes of Jacob, and to restore the preserved ones of Israel; I* **will also give You as a light to the Gentiles**, *that You should be My salvation to the ends of the earth"* (Isaiah 49:6).

The Hebrew word for salvation in the last line of verse 6 is *Yeshua*, the name of Jesus. This Scripture from Isaiah was spoken concerning Jesus in the first days of His life. His parents brought Him to the temple for dedication, and Simeon thanked God and prophesied over Jesus saying:

> *For my eyes have seen Your salvation which You have prepared before the face of all peoples, **a light to bring revelation to the Gentiles**, and the glory of Your people Israel* (Luke 2:30-32).

This same powerful prophecy from the mouth of Isaiah had an important part in Paul's calling as a Messianic Jewish apostle, sent by God to the nations. On his first missionary journey, he preached to a mixed crowd of Jews and Gentiles at Pisidian Antioch and said:

> For so the Lord has commanded us: "*I have set you as a light to the Gentiles*, that you should be for salvation to the ends of the earth" (Acts 13:47).

Modern Messianic Jews are part of a movement that has been visible to the Church for less than a generation. The search for an authentic Jewish identity that is consistent with the whole Bible is an important element in Messianic Jewish life. However, God did not choose Israel to be a light unto itself. It is in serving as a light to the other nations that Israel will find her destiny. God has not rejected Israel, and His chosen purposes for the nation still stand. However, Jesus said, "... *For everyone to whom much is given, from him much will be required; and to whom much has been committed, of him they will ask the more*" (Luke 12:48). The correct response to being chosen by God is a deep sense of obligation. Knowing the privilege of being chosen without feeling obligation is exclusivity. This was the root sin of the Pharisees, the leading Jewish sect in Jesus' day. Their exclusivity was integral to their hypocrisy. They were chosen by God to be His representatives. They knew God to be the Creator and Lord of the entire world, not just of the Jewish people. They knew the God-given destiny of the Jewish people was to be a blessing to "all the families of the earth." In spite of this knowledge, they selfishly blocked the way for others to enter into the Kingdom of God. Jesus said to them:

> But woe to you, scribes and Pharisees, hypocrites! For you shut up the kingdom of heaven against men; for you neither go in yourselves, nor do you allow those who are entering to go in (Matthew 23:13).

Jesus told His own Jewish disciples not to be like the Pharisees. His disciples had to learn that the greatest among them would have to be the servant of all. By "all" He evidently meant both Jews and Gentiles. Jesus' ministry involved cross-cultural evangelism from the start. In Galilee, Jesus gave His disciples the Great Commission to "go into all the world," years before the Jerusalem Council meeting took place as recorded in Acts, chapter 15. He taught the parable of the "Good Samaritan" and deliberately went to a Samaritan woman at the well. He called His conversation with her "the will of Him who sent Me." (See John 4:34.) In His hometown of Nazareth, He taught about Elijah's ministry to the Sidonian widow and about Elisha's ministry to Naaman, the Syrian, even when He knew the teaching would offend his family's friends and neighbors.

The first part of Jesus' sermon in Nazareth was a Messianic proclamation. After this, the people were speaking well of Him and wondering at the gracious words that were coming from His lips. They apparently had little problem with the idea of the Messiah coming from their own town. However, Jesus was not finished, and He completed his sermon reminding His people of the obligation of the chosen. Their hearts were not only closed to that message, but they reacted angrily.

> *"But I tell you truly, many widows were in Israel in the days of Elijah, when the heaven was shut up three years and six months, and there was a great famine throughout all the land; but to none of them was Elijah sent except to Zarephath, in the region of Sidon, to a woman who was a widow. And many lepers were in Israel in the time of Elisha the prophet, and none of them was cleansed except Naaman the Syrian." So **all those in the synagogue, when they heard these things, were filled with wrath,** and rose up and thrust Him out of the city; and they led Him to the brow of the hill on which their*

city was built, that they might throw Him down over the cliff (Luke 4:25-29).

Jesus was always clear about God's ultimate intention to reach every nation with the good news of His kingdom. The great temple in Jerusalem was the dwelling place of God on Earth. It had an outer court called the "Court of the Gentiles" that was meant as a place for non-Jews to worship. When Jesus cleared the temple of its buyers and sellers, He was objecting to what they were doing as much as He was angered by where they were conducting their commerce. The sellers of sacrificial animals and the changers of money were encroaching on the Court of the Gentiles and obstructing them from entering into prayer and worship of the one true God.

> *So they came to Jerusalem. And Jesus went into the temple and began to drive out those who bought and sold in the temple, and overturned the tables of the money changers and the seats of those who sold doves. And He would not allow anyone to carry wares through the temple. Then He taught, saying to them, "Is it not written, 'My house shall be called a house of prayer for all nations?' But you have made it a 'den of thieves'"* (Mark 11:15-17).

The Scripture that Jesus quoted from Isaiah is specifically about foreigners worshipping among the people of Israel at the temple. Here is the full text that most of the Jewish merchants in the temple must have known:

> *Also the sons of the foreigner who join themselves to the LORD, to serve Him, and to love the name of the LORD, to be His servants—everyone who keeps from defiling the Sabbath, and holds fast My covenant even them I will bring to My holy mountain, and make*

*them joyful in My house of prayer. Their burnt offerings and their sacrifices will be accepted on My altar; for **My house shall be called a house of prayer for all nations*** (Isaiah 56:6-7)

In the early days of the Church, no one did more to spread the message of Jesus to the Gentiles than Paul. He understood himself to be doubly chosen by God, first as a Jew and secondly, as a believer. In addition to having received the gift of eternal life through faith in Jesus, Paul understood that being Jewish was a great advantage. (See Romans 3:1-3.) These advantages led him to a sense of debt toward those less advantaged. He wrote about his obligation that was specifically toward the Gentiles. It was his deep sense of spiritual indebtedness that was a driving force of his ministry.

> *I am a debtor both to Greeks and to barbarians, both to wise and to unwise. So, as much as is in me, I am ready to preach the gospel to you who are in Rome also* (Romans 1:14-15).

Paul's aim was not to annihilate Jewish identity or Torah-observance, but to indicate a greater truth that went beyond the covenant that God made at Mt. Sinai. Revealing this truth to the nations was his call, and by extension, part of the specific call given to the Messianic Jews of today. Paul saw a truth higher and greater than national, religious, or cultural identity. Toward the end of his ministry, he said he was "not disobedient to the heavenly vision." Although Paul always understood himself to be a Jew by God's sovereign choice, his eternal identity was anchored in Heaven—not in Jewishness. Because he understood the great value of being Jewish, Paul's sacrifice of this identity became all the more significant. Inspired by the Holy Spirit, he wrote:

Though I also might have confidence in the flesh. If anyone else thinks he may have confidence in the flesh, I more so: circumcised the eighth day, of the stock of Israel, of the tribe of Benjamin, **a Hebrew of the Hebrews;** *concerning the law, a Pharisee; concerning zeal, persecuting the church; concerning the righteousness which is in the law, blameless.* **But what things were gain to me, these I have counted loss for Christ.** *Yet indeed I also count all things loss for the excellence of the knowledge of Christ Jesus my Lord, for whom I have suffered the loss of all things, and count them as rubbish, that I may gain Christ* (Philippians 3:4-8).

Paul wasn't under the divine law of the Torah that defined his people as a nation under God. He had "died to the Law." (See Galatians 2:19.) This spiritual death in identification with Jesus' crucifixion meant spiritual freedom for Paul. It meant freedom to transcend his Jewishness to become "all things to all men" in order to bring them to the Lord. As we read his words, we can feel his zeal and powerful sense of obligation. Because of the liberty he found in faith, and because he understood himself to be specially chosen by God (as a Jew, a believer, and an apostle), Paul made himself a slave to all for the sake of the Lord.

For though I am free from all men, I have made myself a servant to all, that I might win the more; *and to the Jews I became as a Jew, that I might win Jews; to those who are under the law, as under the law, that I might win those who are under the law; to those who are without law, as without law (not being without law toward God, but under law toward Christ), that I might win those who are without law; to the weak I became as weak, that I might win the weak. I have* **become all things to all men, that I might by all means save some** (1 Corinthians 9:19-22).

Jonah Represents Israel

In the Bible, an individual man often serves as God's picture of a nation. Abraham was called the "Father of Many Nations." David, son of Jesse, represented Israel as her king. On *Yom Kippur* (Day of Atonement), the holiest and most solemn of Israel's holidays, the book of Jonah is traditionally read in the synagogues as the *Haftarah* reading. The story of Jonah prophetically expresses the story of Israel, and we can see God's choosing of a man and God's choosing of a nation.

In Jonah, chapter one, the word of God came to Jonah the first time. God said, *"Arise, go to Nineveh, that great city, and cry out against it; for their wickedness has come up before Me"* (Jonah 1:2). This is a picture of God's purpose in His original covenant with Israel. God chose Israel to be a light to all the nations, but Israel chose not to be chosen and rejected God's call. In the book of Jonah, the prophet arose, but not to go and preach. Jonah disobeyed and fled by ship, but God caused a violent storm, and each Gentile sailor in desperation called upon his own god. When the sailors found out that Jonah, a Jew, was fleeing in disobedience to God, they were astonished. They did not really trust in their own gods and only prayed when they were in trouble. Here was a Jew. How could he disobey the true and living God?

> *Then they said to him, "Please tell us! For whose cause is this trouble upon us? What is your occupation? And where do you come from? What is your country? And of what people are you?" So he said to them, "I am a Hebrew; and I fear the LORD, the God of heaven, who made the sea and the dry land." Then the men were exceedingly afraid, and said to him, "**Why have you done this?**" For the men knew that he fled from the presence of the LORD, because he had told them* (Jonah 1:8-10).

123

Jonah accepted the blame for the ship's misfortune and was thrown into the sea. In the same way, we see the nations raging in fearful frustration and a shadow of future anti-Semitism, as the Jew in the midst of the nations is identified and cast out to his death. God appointed a fish to swallow Jonah. It was a sea monster of judgment and near extinction, but also the vessel of Jonah's ultimate preservation.

Jesus, the greatest of teachers, explained this mysterious event:

> *An evil and adulterous generation seeks after a sign, and no sign will be given to it except **the sign of the prophet Jonah**. For as Jonah was three days and three nights in the belly of the great fish, so will the Son of Man be three days and three nights in the heart of the earth* (Matthew 12:39-40).

Throughout the Bible, the phrase "depths of the sea" is a symbol of judgment, death, and separation from God. In one of Jesus' sternest warnings He said:

> *But whoever causes one of these little ones who believe in Me to sin, it would be better for him if a millstone were hung around his neck, and he were drowned in the depth of the sea* (Matthew 18:6).

Jesus compared Jonah's sojourn in the depths of the sea with His own journey to the place of death and separation from God. For Israel's Messiah to be crucified meant death not just for Him alone, but judgment and destruction for the entire nation. You may remember what Jesus said as many gathered to weep and lament as they watched Him on His way to the Cross.

> *But Jesus, turning to them, said, "Daughters of Jerusalem, do not weep for Me, but weep for yourselves and for your children ... For if they do these things in*

the green wood, what will be done in the dry?" (Luke 23:28; 31).

After 70 A.D., most of the people of Israel were expelled from the land of their inheritance, and Israel ceased to function as a nation. What followed was almost two thousand years of wanderings, persecutions, expulsions, and murders, culminating in the Holocaust when European Jews were systematically hunted down and exterminated. However, in 1948, the modern State of Israel was born. Even as Jesus died and was resurrected to new life, the nation of Israel disappeared from the Earth to be reborn in our time. The appearance of modern Messianic Jewish believers in Israel today is a *resurrection* of the faith held by the first Israeli disciples of Jesus.

In Jonah, chapter 3 we are told, *"The word of the Lord came to Jonah a second time."* God is the "Lord of the second chance," and His second call to Jonah was exactly the same as His first—Go, preach to another nation. This time Jonah obeyed the word of God and became Israel's best-known, cross-cultural prophet—a Jewish man sent as a light to the nations. In our day, we are witnessing not only the historic return of the Jewish people to the land of Israel, but also the rise of indigenous Israeli congregations that worship Jesus in the very land where He once walked. God is sending His Word a second time to the Messianic believers of Israel in order to fulfill the chosen nation's call. Jonah was a Jewish prophet sent to bless the traditional enemies of his own people. Modern Israel's redemption as a nation is joined with her calling to be a light, bringing Jesus' message of salvation to the Arabs and other peoples of the world. Paul the Apostle wrote, *"… blindness in part has happened to Israel **until the fullness of the Gentiles has come in**. And so all Israel will be saved.…"* (Romans 11:25b-26a).

There is a majestic sequence to God's actions in history, and a unique season given for each nation. Many nations receive only one historic opportunity to be a light to the world—one season of God's special visitation, however long or short that may be. If that opportunity is seized, a nation may be transformed, and a lasting spiritual heritage imparted. If God's moment is missed, the blessing is lost and cannot be regained except through widespread repentance and waiting upon God. The Bible says, however, that the Lord will give the remnant of Israel a second and final chance. Modern Israeli believers have an important role in the salvation of the Gentiles and as a witness to all the nations.

Sadly, in the fourth chapter of Jonah, the prophet is described as angry and depressed after God's merciful treatment of repentant Nineveh. Jonah had preached to the people of the city, but he simply did not love them with God's kind of love. He had learned to be obedient, but his heart had not been deeply changed. The transformation of character that is necessary for such a change of heart, whether in a prophet or in an entire nation, can only be accomplished through the sacrificial ministry of Jesus, the Son of God.

Simon, the Son of Jonah

God's concern is the salvation of the entire human race. Jesus never shrank from the universal aspect of the call to salvation. However, in spite of the intended international application of His message, Jesus' ministry was personal and focused on the few. Reading through the New Testament, we see that Jesus was surrounded by concentric rings of humanity. Beginning with the outside and moving inwardly, there were the unknowing and hopeless nations of the world, then the unbelieving Israeli masses, the mildly interested crowds, the camp followers and the needy, the seventy disciples, the twelve chosen apostles, the inner three—Peter, James and John—and finally Peter, a leader among the disciples.

It is clear that Jesus spent the bulk of His time and attention training the twelve Jewish men who had been selected for Him by God. The inner three were set apart for specific revelation and assignments, such as accompanying Jesus up the mountain of transfiguration or praying close to Him in the Garden of Gethsemane. Peter is characterized as the leader of this inner group, and he was singled out for special attention from the Lord on numerous occasions. One day, while with His disciples in the remote northern region of Israel, Jesus asked them, *"Who do you say that I am?"*

> *Simon Peter answered and said: "You are the Christ, the Son of the living God." Jesus answered and said to him, "Blessed are you, **Simon Bar-Jonah**, for flesh and blood has not revealed this to you, but My Father who is in heaven. **And I also say to you that you are Peter**, and on this rock I will build My church, and the gates of Hades shall not prevail against it. And I will give you the keys of the kingdom of heaven, and whatever you bind on earth will be bound in heaven, and whatever you loose on earth will be loosed in heaven"* (Matthew 16:16-19).

At that moment, after having received divine revelation about Jesus, Peter was given a new name—his own eternal identity. Jesus called him a rock! His new identity was to be rooted in a Christ-like character of strength and stability. Although he was boastful, impulsive, and unreliable, he would become a foundation-laying apostle, commanding tremendous authority and respect. Furthermore, Jesus gave him the keys to the Kingdom of Heaven—symbols of new authority and power from God for the work of his future ministry.

After the testing of Peter's faith and the resurrection of Jesus, Peter was transformed from Simon Bar-Jonah (Simon, the son of Jonah) into a mighty man of God. He used both of the kingdom keys given to him by Jesus to open the door of salvation to Israel and the nations. The first key was used when he preached in Jerusalem on the day of Pentecost. Three thousand Jews were saved that day, and the first Messianic congregation was begun in Israel. Peter used the second key when he obeyed God's vision (recorded in Acts, chapter 10), defied the restrictions of his own Jewish culture, and went to Caesarea to preach to the Gentiles. Later, Paul would become better known for His ministry to the Gentiles, but Peter was the pioneer, the first Jewish apostle to hear, obey, and go. On that day in Caesarea, Peter said, *"In truth I perceive that God shows no partiality. But in every nation whoever fears Him and works righteousness is accepted by Him"* (Acts 10:34-35). When Peter saw the Holy Spirit fall upon the Gentiles for the first time, he had the presence of mind and the God-given authority to command that they be baptized in water immediately.

For Zion's Sake

God's original covenant purpose and call for Israel and the Jewish people to be a spiritual light to all nations has not changed. The love of God for Israel's Arab neighbors and for all nations demonstrates the true light of the Messiah. Today, in the modern state, a remnant of Israeli believers is worshipping Jesus and bringing the power of His Spirit back home to Israel after almost two thousand years. New Messianic congregations are springing up in various places. Among the steadily growing numbers of Jewish believers are individuals and families who are called to reach out to the Arab world and to all nations. It is for Zion's sake—for the salvation of Israel, as well as for the world, that they obey and preach to other cultures. Answering the Lord's call, these "sons of Jonah" are being transformed into modern Peters—men and women of courage and authority who are launching out into God's end-time harvest throughout the world.

For Zion's sake I will not hold My peace, and for Jerusalem's sake I will not rest, until her righteousness goes forth as brightness, and her salvation as a lamp *that burns. **The Gentiles shall see your righteousness,** and all kings your glory. You shall be called by a new name, which the mouth of the LORD will name* (Isaiah 62:1-2).

The One New Man

Increasingly, the world is being confronted with the effects of conflict between Jews and Arabs. A state of war has existed between Israel and much of the Arab world ever since the founding of the state in 1948. This ongoing conflict and the tension that is rooted in it now threatens the political stability of the entire planet. Almost twenty centuries after the New Testament was written, we are beginning to appreciate again the full impact of what was written about Jew and Gentile becoming one in the Messiah. Paul wrote the following to the mostly Gentile church in Ephesus:

> *For He Himself is our peace, who has made both* [Jews and Gentiles] *one, and has **broken down the middle wall of separation,** having abolished in His flesh the enmity, that is, the law of commandments contained in ordinances, **so as to create in Himself one new man from the two, thus making peace*** (Ephesians 2:14-15).

The original language of this "one new man" describes something complete, fresh, and previously unseen. It is a wholeness that does not deny or destroy the distinctive nature and unique gifting of the parts. To the Galatians, Paul wrote:

> *For as many of you as were baptized into Christ have put on Christ. **There is neither Jew nor Greek,** there is neither slave nor free, **there is neither male nor female;** for you are all one in Christ Jesus* (Galatians 3:27-28).

Yes, there is genuine unity between Jews and Gentiles through Messianic faith. On the other hand, the distinctiveness of God's unique work within each people group and each group's special calling is preserved. In the same verse, Paul uses the division between men and women in a parallel manner. No one would suggest that he meant believers should ignore the obvious and God-given distinctiveness of the genders. The church is not to be a single *homogenized* body, but rather a fascinating display of diversity brought together by a common Spirit. The Body of Christ has many distinct members, but only one Head.

God meant for Jews and Arabs to live together in the land of Israel. However, in order for this to become a political reality, the right of Jews to the land they were promised should be recognized. The land of Israel was a divine gift to Abraham, and God meant it to be passed on through Isaac and Jacob to the twelve tribes of Israel. The New Testament affirms God's commitment to this inheritance. Paul wrote that even in their rejection of the gospel, the Jewish people still retain God's promises.

> *Concerning the gospel they are enemies for your sake, but concerning the election they are beloved for the sake of the fathers. **For the gifts and the calling of God are irrevocable*** (Romans 11:28-29).

Arabs who accept the *nation* of Israel's right to exist in the *land* of Israel, can live alongside the Jewish people, and share in this inheritance. The unity of Jew and Gentile extends to the inheritance of the land given to Israel. The great prophet Ezekiel spoke out about Gentiles who join themselves to the people of Israel and dwell with them in the land.

> *"Thus you shall divide this land among yourselves according to the tribes of Israel. It shall be that you will*

> *divide it by lot as an inheritance for yourselves, and for the strangers who dwell among you and who bear children among you.* ***They shall be to you as native-born among the children of Israel; they shall have an inheritance with you among the tribes of Israel.*** *And it shall be that in whatever tribe the stranger dwells,* ***there you shall give him his inheritance,***" *says the Lord God* (Ezekiel 47:21-23).

My ancestors are from Japan, and although my people do not have the same family history with Israel as the Arabs, I am a Gentile like those described by Ezekiel. In 1987, I came to live alongside the Jewish people in the land of Israel's inheritance. My son was born on Mount Carmel in 1989. Since my wife is Jewish, our children are considered Jewish by Israeli law. That means I am the only Gentile in the family! According to God's Word, I have been given an inheritance in the land of Israel alongside the native born.

This is God's "road map" to peace in the Middle East. Arabs and Jews can live together in the land in peace if the Prince of Peace is ruling in their hearts. Scripturally, our citizenship is in Heaven, and God has called Jews, Arabs, and other Gentiles to a place of unity in God's kingdom. In Psalm 122, the Spirit of God commands us to "pray for the peace of Jerusalem." There is no better road to peace in Jerusalem than by lifting up the name of Jesus. He is "the way, the truth and the life." There is no other way to peace.

The name Jerusalem means "city of peace," and in Hebrew, the word is plural. It literally means "two Jerusalems." We know from the Book of Revelation that there is to be a New Jerusalem coming down out of Heaven from God, and this is a picture of God's kingdom coming to Earth in its fullness. Paul also wrote about two Jerusalems to the Galatian church. He compares the first, earthly Jerusalem, to the covenant of the law. His picture of the law is associated with Hagar, the mother of Ishmael and

Arabia. The Jerusalem of the New Covenant is from above and is free. This is the city where Jesus reigns as King of Kings. Believers must learn to walk in the earthly city as citizens of the heavenly one.

> *For it is written that **Abraham had two sons: the one by a bondwoman, the other by a freewoman**. But he who was of the bondwoman was born according to the flesh, and he of the freewoman through promise, which things are symbolic. For these are the two covenants: the one from Mount Sinai which gives birth to bondage, which is Hagar—for this **Hagar is Mount Sinai in Arabia, and corresponds to Jerusalem which now is**, and is in bondage with her children—but the **Jerusalem above is free, which is the mother of us all*** (Galatians 4:22-26).

When Jesus ministered in Jerusalem, He wept over the city and gave a condition for His return. Today, in many Messianic fellowships we sing, *"Baruch haba b' shem Adonai,"* which means, "Blessed is He who comes in the name of the Lord." We sing that song as an intercessory prayer for Jerusalem, and for the Lord's return to heal the heart of this city that is bitterly divided between Jews and Arabs.

> *O Jerusalem, Jerusalem, the one who kills the prophets and stones those who are sent to her! How often I wanted to gather your children together, as a hen gathers her chicks under her wings, but you were not willing! See! Your house is left to you desolate; for I say to you, you shall see Me no more till you say, **"Blessed is He who comes in the name of the LORD!"*** (Matthew 23:37-39).

God's plan for the Middle East includes revival and genuine reconciliation between Jews and Arabs. Messianic Jewish congregations are growing in Israel. As revival stirs in the Arab world, former Muslims are coming into the Kingdom of God. We are seeing the establishment of a powerful testimony of unity in Christ as Messianic Jews and Arab Christians are drawn together by a common faith in Jesus. Their testimony is destined to impact the world. Where today there are armed barricades, minefields, and borders, God says there is to be a thoroughfare of His purposes in the Middle East. Pray with us for revival, reconciliation, and for this highway to be built on the Lord's road map for peace in the region.

In that day there will be a highway from Egypt to Assyria, and the Assyrian will come into Egypt and the Egyptian into Assyria, and the Egyptians will serve with the Assyrians. In that day Israel will be one of three with Egypt and Assyria—a blessing in the midst of the land, whom the LORD of hosts shall bless, saying, "Blessed is Egypt My people, and Assyria the work of My hands, and Israel My inheritance" (Isaiah 19:23-25).

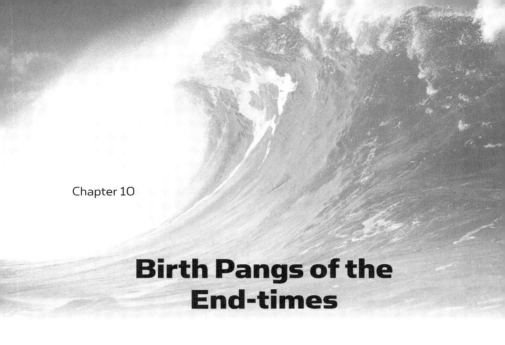

Chapter 10

Birth Pangs of the End-times

JESUS' OWN DISCIPLES APPROACHED HIM privately on the Mount of Olives and asked about the signs of His return. His direct answer as recorded by Matthew must form the basis of our beliefs concerning the end-times.

> *Now as He sat on the Mount of Olives, the disciples came to Him privately, saying, "Tell us, when will these things be? And what will be the sign of Your coming, and of the end of the age?" And Jesus answered and said to them: "**Take heed that no one deceives you.** For many will come in My name, saying, 'I am the Christ,' and will deceive many. **And you will hear of wars and rumors of wars. See that you are not troubled; for all these things must come to pass, but the end is not yet.** For nation will rise against nation, and kingdom against kingdom. And there will be famines, pestilences, and earthquakes in various places. **All these are the beginning of [birth pangs] sorrows**"* (Matthew 24:3-8).

Jesus said that the days before His return would be characterized by deception and false messiahs. Today, the greatest challenge to the gospel is coming from the Islamic world. Muslims believe that the "prophet like Moses," mentioned in Deuteronomy, chapter 18, is Mohammed. Also, it is written in the Koran that when Jesus promised to send the Holy Spirit, He was referring to the prophet Mohammed. Islam forbids worship of Jesus and declares that God has no son.

Jesus also predicted "wars and rumors of wars." We are in that period now. The twentieth century had more devastation through war than all the previous centuries of human history put together. Anyone who thinks the twenty-first century will have fewer wars is unrealistically optimistic. The world has come through a war in Afghanistan and another in Iraq. The Iraq war followed a long and difficult "rumor" of war that lasted almost half a year.

Today, famine stalks sub-Sahara Africa and areas of Asia including North Korea. Our modern world has been stricken with new pestilences—HIV/AIDS and deadly viruses with names like West Nile, Ebola, and SARS. Although the number of major earthquakes per year throughout the world does not appear to be increasing, the number of people killed by earthquakes each year is growing significantly. This is because more and more people are living in cities, and urban areas are more susceptible to killer quakes. In rural areas, the population is less dense and houses are built closer to the ground. According to Jesus' words in Matthew, chapter 24, these are all signs of the end-times.

In spite of these frightening events, Jesus said we should not be troubled. It is not yet the end. These events are just the beginning of travail that will bring the Kingdom of God into full view. The Greek word used in Matthew 24:7 translated "sorrows" is the word *odin* which means "birth pang." Mothers know that birth pangs begin with mild contractions and long periods of quiet in between. As the time of birth approaches, the pains increase in intensity and frequency. A woman is strengthened in labor as she looks forward to the birth of her child, and doesn't focus on the pain. So it is with these times. We are experiencing "birth pangs," and God is bringing something wonderful to life. What "birth" should we look forward to that makes all these difficulties worthwhile?

The Apostle Paul sheds light on the words of Jesus in the eighth chapter of his prophetic letter to the Roman church:

> For I consider that the sufferings of this present time are not worthy to be compared with the glory which shall be revealed in us. **For the earnest expectation of the creation eagerly waits for the revealing of the sons of God.** For the creation was subjected to futility, not willingly, but because of Him who subjected it in hope; because the creation itself also will be delivered from the bondage of corruption into the glorious liberty of the children of God. **For we know that the whole creation groans and labors with birth pangs together until now** (Romans 8:18-22).

Paul wrote that the entire creation is groaning with labor pains while waiting for the revelation or manifestation of God's children. The birth that is coming is the revelation of God's Son in the hearts of men and women, and the spiritual transformation of their lives into His image. Having the Spirit of God's Son is what makes us sons and daughters of God. It is not enough to believe that God sent His Son, Jesus, for the redemption of the world. We must also, because of Him, accept our identity as God's offspring and live fully in that new reality. In the same chapter of Romans, Paul also wrote:

> **For you did not receive the spirit of bondage again to fear, but you received the Spirit of adoption by whom we cry out, "Abba, Father."** The Spirit Himself bears

witness with our spirit that we are children of God, and if children, then heirs—heirs of God and joint heirs with Christ, if indeed we suffer with Him, that we may also be glorified together (Romans 8:15-17).

There is a corporate dimension to what Paul has written. The complete revealing of God's offspring requires that people from every nation, tribe, and tongue be represented. Then the whole Body of Christ can be fully seen. This is the weight behind Jesus' words in Matthew 24:14, "*And this gospel of the kingdom will be preached in all the world as a witness to all the nations, and then the end will come.*" This is also the meaning behind God's insistence that the "*fullness of the Gentiles*" must come in before "*all Israel will be saved.*" (See Romans 11:25-26.) This "fullness" doesn't simply mean masses of people and numbers of unreached ethnic groups, but also a heretofore unattained level of spiritual maturity and unity in the Body of Christ. Through the suffering brought about by wars and persecution, the true Church throughout the world is being prepared and thrust into the light of God's presence. The Bride of Christ is being made ready.

> *... till **we all** come to the unity of the faith and of the knowledge of the Son of God, to a perfect [complete] man, **to the measure of the stature of the fullness of [Messiah]*** (Ephesians 4:13).

There is a new church emerging that is "designed" by God for growth in these end-times. This new worldwide body of believers is in the process of shedding the remnants of "old wineskin" religious tradition left over from movements that sprung out of the Reformation almost five hundred years ago. Part of God's tsunami of change, this new movement includes the following characteristics:

1. It has a prophetic understanding of Israel's significance in the end-times and is a "one new man" body of Jews and Gentiles worshipping in unity.

2. It has a vision for outreach focused on the unreached portion of the world. Integral to this vision for outreach is Jesus' command to teach and "make disciples" of the nations, not to simply multiply church gatherings.

3. It is non-denominational, that is, not bound by ecclesiastical hierarchies, or institutionalized lines of authority.

4. Genuine apostolic and prophetic leaders with authority beyond their own local communities are recognized because of their spiritual gifting, proven character, and the tested results of their ministries.

5. It is networked with local and national assemblies of similar vision throughout the world.

6. There is no artificial division between sacred and secular callings. All genuine vocations in the Church are honored as God-given and anointed for building His Kingdom. This is essential for the Church to be a transforming agent in society.

7. It is a body actively pursuing peace with God and man with worship, prayer, and discipleship considered its highest earthly responsibilities.

Arabian Night

As the gospel makes its way across Asia from east to west, conflict with dark spiritual strongholds will be reflected in the political realm. The world has already entered a new and violent process of political realignment. The World Trade Center and Pentagon attacks, the subsequent war in Afghanistan and then in Iraq are a trail of conflict that is related to God's end-time plans. It is my opinion that this path of conflict will eventually lead to the heart of the Arab world and Saudi Arabia. The ensuing battles will come suddenly and will have serious negative consequences on the economy and politics of the world. I believe Isaiah prophesied about this coming war, and then specifically mentioned a confrontation in Arabia between local tribal factions. This coming conflict is another birth pang or "contraction" of the end-times.

> *Therefore my loins are filled with pain;* **pangs have taken hold of me, like the pangs of a woman in labor.** *I was distressed when I heard it; I was dismayed when I saw it* (Isaiah 21:3).

Later, in this same chapter, the prophet wrote of war in Arabia. The names Dumah, Tema, and Kedar are all sons of Ishmael, and Dedan and Seir are names associated with Esau in the Bible. These are the tribes that comprise the Arab peoples today.

> *The burden against Dumah. He calls to me out of Seir, "Watchman, what of the night? Watchman, what of the night?" The watchman said, "The morning comes, and also the night. If you will inquire, inquire; return! Come back!"*

> **The burden against Arabia.** *In the forest in Arabia you will lodge, O you traveling companies of Dedanites. O inhabitants of the land of Tema, bring water to him who is thirsty; with their bread they met him who fled. For* **they fled from the swords, from the drawn sword, from the bent bow, and from the distress of war.** *For thus the LORD has said to me: "Within a year, according to the year of a hired man,* **all the glory of Kedar will fail;** *and the remainder of the number of archers, the mighty men of the people of Kedar, will be diminished; for the LORD God of Israel has spoken it"* (Isaiah 21:11-17).

I believe that Isaiah's prediction has an application for today. In the not so distant future, Saudi Arabia's oil-producing facilities could be destroyed or rendered useless by a spreading Middle East conflict. Saudi Arabia is the heart of the Muslim faith having both holy cities of Mecca and Medina within its borders. It is the home of the radical Wahabi Muslim sect that produced Osama Bin Laden and fifteen of the nineteen hijackers in the World Trade Center and Pentagon suicide attacks. Saudi Arabia is also the most influential oil producing nation since it has the world's largest reserves and the highest quality of crude oil. Today, it is the only oil producing country with significant excess pumping capacity. This means that Saudi Arabia holds a place of powerful influence among the oil producing and exporting nations of the world. These nations can stabilize, and to a certain extent control, the world oil price by putting more or less oil on the market at any given time.

Although the United States has massive emergency oil reserves and is dependent for only about 10 percent of its oil from the Middle East, other industrialized countries in Western Europe and Asia, including Japan, are vitally linked to oil from that region. In today's global economy, a crisis that involves one major country affects everyone. A war between Israel and the Islamic Republic of Iran would immediately close the Strait of Hormuz to its vital traffic of oil tankers. This disruption to the flow of oil to the industrialized world could have a devastating effect on the global economy. For this reason, military intervention from the United States and her allies would be inevitable. These would certainly be decisive events of today's growing conflict with the spiritual "principality" of Islam. The political and spiritual fragmentation of Islamic authority that is already in progress will continue and accelerate. As a result, in the future we will see a great movement among the people of Central Asia and the Middle East toward the gospel. These events and the political upheavals that surround them will shake the Earth and accelerate the tsunami of the Lord's purposes in the last days.

Standing With Israel

In the midst of a troubled and violent world, the purpose of the Church is to worship God and to be an earthly witness, standing in demonstration of His will in each generation. The most significant and enduring political conflict in our world today is related to the existence of the State of Israel. In spite of the desperate need for peacemaking and justice in the Middle East, the issue of Israel's existence and legitimacy as a Jewish homeland is a crucial matter for Christians to understand. There are a myriad of political, social, and economic issues at stake in the Middle East. However, before we can address these pressing issues, we have to come to terms with the spiritual reasons for Israel's existence. Many in the Muslim world believe that the existence of Israel is a huge mistake that needs to be eradicated by any means possible, including military action. At some point, every Christian will have to decide whether to stand for Israel or against it. If conflict involving Israel in the Middle East has a very negative effect on Western economies, a resurgence of anti-Semitism could occur with surprising results.

Standing with Israel does not mean giving blanket endorsement to all the policies of the Israeli government. Israel today is not a godly nation. Today, the remnant of Israeli Messianic believers struggle for recognition in Israel and endure harassment from ultra-orthodox Jews. Messianic Jews work and pray for revival and God's righteousness that is yet to come to this nation. In spite of many national shortcomings and sins, God's mercy and His purposes for the nation will endure. Standing with Israel means prophetically proclaiming this nation's identity in God's plan for the world, and protecting Israel's right to exist in security and peace.

Redemptive Love, Not Romanticism

Many Christians who want to respond positively to God's call to stand with Israel fail to understand that a clear distinction must be made between redeemed Israel that is, Messianic Jews, and religious Judaism. The goal of Messianic Jews is the salvation of all Israel, but the dream of many religious Jews is to rebuild the temple in Jerusalem so that all the Old Testament laws can be fulfilled. In the much more distant future, the day will come when Islam is no longer a threat to Israel. The principality of Islam will be humbled, its power to intimidate will be broken, and millions of former Muslims will find their way into the Kingdom of God. At that time, with the restraining principality of Islam weakened, the spirit of ultra-orthodox Judaism will finally have the opportunity to fulfill its destiny. A third temple will be built on the Temple Mount. Laws restricting true freedom of religion will be strengthened, and Messianic believers will be persecuted harshly. The institutional or traditional church along, with New Age spiritual movements from all over the world, will ally themselves with the ultra-orthodox Jews in a counterfeit "one new man." This false alliance is against God's purposes because it will be unity for the sake of unity, not for the glory of God. Jesus will not be the center of it. There will be no sacrifice of the Cross breaking down dividing walls in the heart. The end-time, apostate church will have no desire to see Jews spiritually reborn. This false reconciliation between Jews and Christians will be like building a temporary bridge between two man-made islands rather than a bold joining of nations through shared, sacrificial, Messianic faith.

As we progress deeper into the end-times, tell-tale characteristics of the spirit of anti-Christ will become more obvious. Evil spiritual forces will increasingly oppose and oppress Israeli Messianic believers in Jesus. The Body of the Messiah in Israel is God's seed of redemption for the whole nation. Only as local fellowships grow will the witness of Jesus in this nation become more visible and influential. Israeli believers are needed as "salt and light" in business and government, education and the arts, sports and entertainment, as well as in pulpit ministries. Israel is "rocky soil" for the gospel today. Believers are less than half of one percent of the total population. Legislation specifically curtailing the freedom of Israelis to share Messianic beliefs has been debated in Israel's Knesset (national assembly). Four separate attempts to pass laws against sharing the gospel with adults have been shelved solely because of international pressure on the Israeli government. Messianic Jewish believers who witness on the streets have been harassed and physically threatened by ultra-orthodox youths in various parts of the country. The sanctuary of a Messianic congregation in the Haifa area was firebombed—the office was gutted, costly electronic equipment melted, and extensive smoke damage occurred. A believer in Jerusalem was attacked with a knife and seriously wounded while passing out invitations to receive a free video of the film, *Jesus*. In 2008, the fifteen-year-old son of Messianic believers was seriously injured when what he thought was a Purim gift for the family turned out to be a bomb.

Through persecution and the purifying fire of God's visitation, and through the steady increase in the number of Israeli believers, a time of national revival is coming to this land. Standing with Israel means encouraging the growth of local Messianic congregations and supporting their right to worship freely and preach the gospel in the modern State of Israel.

And so all Israel will be saved, as it is written: "The Deliverer will come out of Zion, and He will turn away ungodliness from Jacob; for this is My covenant with them, when I take away their sins" (Romans 11:26-27).

Chapter 11

Restoration and Revival

AS WE SURVEY THE LANDSCAPE of end-time events, it is clear that there will be a spiritual restoration of biblical truth that will precede the return of the Lord. Jesus said that the spirit and power of Elijah was part of this restoration. He identified Elijah's ministry with the work and person of John the Baptist.

> *Jesus answered and said to them, "Indeed, **Elijah is coming first and will restore all things**. But I say to you that Elijah has come already, and they did not know him but did to him whatever they wished. Likewise the Son of Man is also about to suffer at their hands." Then the disciples understood that He spoke to them of John the Baptist* (Matthew 17:11-13).

Malachi's prophecy, however, speaks of Elijah's restoration coming before "the great and dreadful day of the Lord." This means that just as John the Baptist ministered in Elijah's spirit and power to prepare the way for Jesus' first coming, there is to be another release of this ministry before Jesus returns to judge the Earth.

Behold, I will send you Elijah the prophet **before the coming of the great and dreadful day of the LORD**. *And he will turn the hearts of the fathers to the children, and the hearts of the children to their fathers, lest I come and strike the earth with a curse* (Malachi 4:5-6).

Turning the hearts of fathers to the children and children to their fathers means restoring the Lord's altar of prayer in the family and in the heart of each nation. God's rulership demands a prophetic stand against immorality, spiritual deception, and modern-day child sacrifice, which is the practice of abortion. Elijah's ministry today is a voice crying out, calling God's people together to rebuild the Lord's altar of sacrificial worship and to turn the heart of their nations back to God.

Europe and the Church of the Future

Has the great tsunami of Christian growth come to Europe and gone never to return? May it never be! God has a plan for yet another age of growth for the Church in Europe. Yes, Europe has some of the oldest Christian history in the world, but being older simply means you are getting closer to the end. All Christians know that the end of history is the return of the Lord. This means that Europe is historically and culturally closer to His return. The evangelical Church in Europe is in fact becoming the Church of the future. The Church in Europe is already facing an anti-Christ spirit that the rest of the world has yet to experience. A generation ago who would have thought that once proud nations like France and Germany would lay down important aspects of their national identities, and even their currencies, to unify under a single secular banner? This is a shadow of the one world anti-Christ system that is one day to come upon all the world. The Church in Europe is struggling against the spiritual oppression of this Goliath today.

Revival in Europe is destined to come from an unexpected yet prophetic source. The verses in Malachi say, *"Elijah the prophet … will restore the hearts of the fathers to their children and the hearts of the children to their fathers"* (Malachi 4:5-6). There was a time in history when European nations seemed to rule the world. Their Christian culture, based on the truths of God's Word, gave them such an advantage that they were able to exercise dominion over many other nations. They used and abused their power during the colonial age. Much has been written and said about the bad that came from that era, but good also came as a result of colonization. Among the good results was that the gospel was preached around the world. William Carey, an eighteenth century Baptist minister from England is recognized as the "father of modern missions."

Today, the spiritual children of the European colonies are coming back to bless their fathers. By this, I mean evangelical Christians from Africa, Latin America, and Asia are returning to Europe in great numbers. They are coming as guest workers and immigrants, and they are coming with a younger, more vibrant, and fresh Christian faith than is native to Europe currently. The prophetic challenge for the Church in Europe today is this: Will the European fathers recognize, accept, and embrace their spiritual children? Will the returning children of the colonies honor their fathers and bring them the gift of Christ's love and new life?

The opportunity God is offering to the new Church in Europe is to be a truly multinational, multi-ethnic body and an example to Christians around the world. The great revivals that are taking place in various parts of the world today where multiplied millions of first generation Christians are pouring into the Kingdom of God in places like Korea, China, Brazil, and Nigeria are primarily *national* movements. While the numbers are impressive and the excitement of new faith is genuine, these movements have a limited impact on the world outside of their own country or region. The new Evangelical/Pentecostal Church in Europe must be genuinely multinational and multi-ethnic, a picture of the diversity and unity in Heaven. This new Church movement will speak with apostolic authority.

Integral to this vision of a new European Church is an understanding of Israel's place in God's end-time plan. How can there be a truly multi-ethnic, end-time Church without the Jewish people? The Jews were originally chosen by God to stand with Him in covenant relationship. The gospel itself is "to the Jew first." After nearly 2000 years, Israel is now a nation in the world again. The number of Messianic Jews, that is, Jews who believe that Jesus is the Messiah is increasing and their presence is visible in the Church today. The modern appearance of Messianic Jews in the Church restores a biblical paradigm, which is the ground and grammar of multi-ethnicity in the Lord's body. According to the Bible, Jews and Gentiles in the Church must be in unity for the Lord's bride to be complete.

Specifically, European Christians should turn from all forms of Replacement Theology and renounce the legacy of Christian anti-Semitism in Europe. Repentance and reconciliation will prepare the way for revival. In today's Europe, it is both possible and vitally important to demonstrate that Messianic Jews and Christian Arabs can be one in the Kingdom of Jesus. The enmity between the families of Isaac and Ishmael has roots that go back to the book of Genesis. The "one new man" of Ephesians, chapter 2, is the cornerstone of the multi-ethnic, multinational new Church in Europe. This is what the apostle Paul meant in Romans, chapter 11, when he wrote that the "fullness" of the Gentiles must come before we will see national revival in Israel. The fullness of the Gentiles means more than just the full number. It also means the fullness of maturity—wholeness that can only come when the Church is truly "one new man" of Jews and all manner of Gentiles together in one body under one King. This is an essential distinguishing mark of the end-time Church. May the new Church in Europe, the Church of the future rise up to this great challenge and in humility take its place of servant leadership, as God's prophetic example to the nations once again.

Mount Carmel

Mount Carmel, the place where Elijah's ministry reached its climax, offers us a picture of prophetic, end-time revival. It is where the prophet confronted the false prophets of Baal and challenged the people of Israel to choose between God and idolatry. In 1955, Bible teacher C. M. Ward wrote, "Mt. Carmel could rightly be called the mount of great decisions." As in the days of Elijah, the world is in a crisis of idolatry and false worship. Mount Carmel again has an important part to play in making ready a people prepared for the Lord. (See Luke 1:17.) This biblical mountain is an elongated range that juts into the Mediterranean Sea on the northwest coast of Israel. The Carmel ridge stretches back from the sea and overlooks the port of Haifa at its northern end and the historic Jezreel valley (Valley of Armageddon) at its southern end. Years before Elijah, in the days of Israel's conquest of the land of Canaan under Joshua, Israel's northern coast was part of the territory allotted to the tribe of Asher. Judges 1:31-32 records that the Asherites never cleared the inhabited coastal areas and that they lived among the Canaanites. By the time of King David, the practice of mingling with the Canaanites had lead to the adoption of their religious practices. Idolatry was widespread. Psalm 106 includes the verses:

> *They did not destroy the peoples, concerning whom the LORD had commanded them, but they mingled with the Gentiles and learned their works; they served their idols, which became a snare to them. They even sacrificed their sons and their daughters to demons, and shed innocent blood, the blood of their sons and daughters, whom they sacrificed to the idols of Canaan;*

and the land was polluted with blood (Psalm 106:34-38).

More than one hundred years after King David, Elijah was a prophet in Israel, and worship of the true God was under attack from all sides. The nation was divided and in steep moral decline under the leadership of weak King Ahab and his evil wife, Jezebel (daughter of a Sidonian king named EthBaal meaning "with Baal"). The high places of the Carmel had become centers of Canaanite Baal and Asherah worship. Israel was under God's judgment, and there were three-and-one-half years of complete drought. This meant economic disaster and famine. God spoke to Elijah and told him to present himself to the King of Israel. When King Ahab saw Elijah, he called God's spokesman a "troubler of Israel." (See I Kings 18:17.) Elijah called for a public confrontation with the false prophets of Baal on Mount Carmel.

When all Israel was gathered on Mount Carmel, Elijah spoke to the people and said, *"How long will you falter between two opinions? If the LORD is God, follow Him; but if Baal, follow him"* (1 Kings 18:21). The people were silent in response to the prophet's challenge. They were unable or unwilling to make a choice to return to the God of Israel. Elijah said to the people, *"I alone am left a prophet of the LORD; but Baal's prophets are four hundred and fifty men"* (I Kings 18:22). Elijah stood alone against evil spiritual forces, social pressures and the threat of personal punishment. He was an example for us all. Everyone who serves the Lord must learn to overcome fear and intimidation. Even if no one agrees with us, the man of God with the Word of God is in the majority.

Elijah said there would be two altars and two sacrifices made. The altar and the sacrifice upon which the fire of God fell would determine the identity of the true God. Now the people were interested enough to agree. This shows that like so many people today, they were an entertainment-oriented culture. There was no heart for a bold decision of faith, but there was certainly enthusiasm for a contest to the death with fire from Heaven. The false prophets of Baal built their altar first. They began to shout and dance around it, but there was not even a flicker of fire from God. Their type of frantic activity is typical of false religion. Leaping around an altar demonstrates no final, lasting commitment.

The Lord's Altar

Genuine altars in the Bible were places where the people of God brought real sacrifices for real blessings. If forgiveness of sin was needed from God, or if a petition or an intercession needed to be heard, the man or woman of Israel came to meet God at the altar. He or she did not come empty-handed. Something living, something of value from their flock or herd was required. Specially trained priests were at the altar to assist in bringing the sacrifice to the Lord. They quickly killed the sacrificial animal and sprinkled its blood on the altar. It was understood that the animal's blood was God's gracious substitute for human life. Because sin resulted in death, there could be no forgiveness without the shedding of blood. (See Leviticus 17:11.) The priests then cut up the sacrifice and placed it on the fire that was burning on the altar. As the sacrifice burned and its smoke rose up into the sky, the Bible says that God accepted it as a sweet-smelling savor. What was sweet to God was not the smell of burning meat. The sweetness was the irrevocable nature of the gift. When the fire had done its work, the sacrifice was gone forever. Sin had been forgiven, and petitions and intercessions had been heard by the Living God.

Biblical altars are for sacrifice, and real sacrifice is meant to be final. God's altars are where people can bring acceptable living sacrifices to the Lord. We give up something of value that represents our life to God, and we don't take it back. Altars are for an exchange of gifts of love between individuals and the Lord. Real love, God's love, makes a final, irrevocable sacrifice. Out of sacrifice, covenant relationship is formed and confirmed. We meet with God at the altar and receive His promise of forgiveness and eternal life. We receive from God healing, wisdom, divine guidance, as well as our chosen calling and spiritual gifts. Our sacrifices to God are non-returnable (they do not come back with us), and we do not leave God's altar the same as when we came.

The pretentious display of the false prophets was a demonstration of false religion, which Elijah mocked. Then the false prophets cut themselves with knives so that the blood ran out upon them. (See I Kings 18:27-29.) They made many little, superficial cuts in the flesh. This also is a feature of false religion. Small cuts in the flesh are trivial sacrifices we make in the place of the great offering that pleases God—our unquestioning obedience. The prophet Samuel once said to the disobedient King Saul:

> Has the LORD as great delight in burnt offerings and sacrifices, as in obeying the voice of the LORD? **Behold, to obey is better than sacrifice**, And to heed than the fat of rams (1 Samuel 15:22).

The small cuts in the flesh are like shallow and false repentances. They are meaningless sacrifices without value to God. The Bible says that the Word of God is a sharp, two-edged sword. It is not for making small cuts in the flesh, but rather for penetrating to the very depth of our being and for putting our sins to death.

> For the word of God is living and powerful, and sharper than any two-edged sword, piercing even to the division of soul and spirit, and of joints and marrow, and is a discerner of the thoughts and intents of the heart (Hebrews 4:12).

When the false prophets had performed all day with their empty and meaningless display, Elijah turned to the people and called out to them. He invited the same people who would not stand with him in the beginning, the same people who only stayed around for a show, to gather around him.

> *Then Elijah said to all the people, "Come near to me." So all the people came near to him. **And he repaired the altar of the LORD that was broken down*** (1 Kings 18:30).

Every time I read these words of the prophet I think of Jesus saying, *"Come to Me, all you who labor and are heavy laden, and I will give you rest"* (Matthew 11:28). In His love, God was reaching out through His prophet to the people of Israel. Then Elijah repaired the altar of the Lord that was broken down. The Hebrew word for repair is *rapha,* which is closer in meaning to the word for healing. He healed the altar that had been nearly destroyed by idolatry in his nation. It was not Elijah's altar, but the Lord's altar in Israel.

Elijah built an altar of twelve stones signifying the twelve tribes or all the people of the Lord. Then he washed the altar three times with water and placed the sacrificial animal on the wood. This is a powerful prophetic foreshadowing of a sacrifice on another mount in Jerusalem generations later. The wood, the bloody flesh, and the water comprise a picture of the sacrifice of Jesus on the Cross. This principle of final, irrevocable sacrifice runs throughout the Bible and is the core of the gospel. New life comes through the obedience of offering the chosen sacrifice to God.

Offering the Sacrifice

Revival is not just a feeling. Revival fire is when sinners get saved, those who have left their faith come back to God, the sick get healed, and even the dead are raised to life. True revival always starts with a powerful return to the Lord. This takes place at the altar of the Cross. The Cross is the ultimate expression of God's love for us. It is the place, the chosen altar, where God himself offered His own Son as a sacrifice for our sins. This Cross is where we meet with a holy God. He has provided the accepted sacrifice for us! It is crucial to believe that God's Son is your sacrifice and the One who has mediated a New Covenant with both Jews and Gentiles. However, there is more to the gospel than simply believing those vitally important facts. Through Jesus' sacrifice, we ourselves become children of God, and in turn, live lives that emulate His. Paul the apostle wrote:

> *I beseech you therefore, brethren, by the mercies of God, that you **present your bodies a living sacrifice**, holy, acceptable to God, which is your reasonable service. And do not be conformed to this world, but be transformed by the renewing of your mind, **that you may prove what is that good and acceptable and perfect will of God*** (Romans 12:1-2).

We follow Jesus by making ourselves a sacrifice too, but we cannot crucify ourselves. Think about it—you may be able to nail one hand down, but that's all. God works this liberating death in our self-centered lives by using our enemies and our environment. Our death to self is so important that God will even use our friends, families, pastors, and teachers. Other people are often God's instruments of our crucifixion. If we recognize the altar of sacrifice and embrace it in the midst of our pain, struggle, suffering, affliction, or difficulty, we will find freedom and be saved. The altar is the end of our suffering because it is the place of death to our flesh, but it is life to the Spirit in us. To embrace suffering and humiliation may seem foolish in the eyes of the world, but God's way is hidden from the proud and is revealed to the humble.

*For the message of the cross is foolishness to those who are perishing, but to us who are being saved it is the power of God.... For Jews request a sign, and Greeks seek after wisdom; but **we preach Christ crucified, to the Jews a stumbling block and to the Greeks foolishness, but to those who are called, both Jews and Greeks, Christ the power of God and the wisdom of God.** Because the foolishness of God is wiser than men, and the weakness of God is stronger than men* (I Corinthians 1:18; 22-25).

The Cross is foolishness, and we are perishing if we say, "Lord, You don't know what they did to me!" or "It's wrong, it's unfair! I quit!" or "Lord, what You are telling me to do is too difficult!" Some people go to the cross with their burdens, but when it begins to really hurt, they get down from it. After a while, it's easy to come down from our cross, and our actions become like the false prophets' trivial cuts in their flesh. Selfish human nature will never be transformed that way. Our fleshly selfishness must die so that the same Spirit that raised Jesus from the dead—the spirit of revival—can come upon us.

After Elijah gathered the people around him at his altar, he prayed a simple and short prayer. The false prophets had taken all day, but Elijah's prayer took no more than a few moments. He had actually spent more time restoring the Lord's altar, and there he prayed for revival.

*And it came to pass, at the time of the offering of the evening sacrifice, that Elijah the prophet came near and said, "LORD God of Abraham, Isaac, and Israel, let it be known this day that You are God in Israel and I am Your servant, and that I have done all these things at Your word. **Hear me, O LORD, hear me, that this people may know that You are the LORD God, and***

that You have turned their hearts back to You again"
(I Kings 18:36-37).

Revival Fire

As soon as the last word of the prophet's prayer left his lips, a mighty flame hurtled down from the sky and consumed the sacrifice and the altar itself. Immediately, the hearts of the people were turned back to God, and they cried out in repentance and worship.

> *Then the fire of the LORD fell and consumed the burnt sacrifice, and the wood and the stones and the dust, and it licked up the water that was in the trench. Now when all the people saw it, they fell on their faces; and they said, "The LORD, He is God!" And Elijah said to them, "Seize the prophets of Baal! Do not let one of them escape!" So they seized them; and Elijah brought them down to the Brook Kishon and executed them there* (I Kings 18:38-40).

I used to think that God had many kinds of fire: fire for judgment, fire for purification, fire for revival, pillars of fire for guidance and worship. Now I realize that there is only one fire of God, and that fire is God himself. The Bible says that God is a consuming fire. (See Hebrews 12:29.) When God comes near, it is both a judgment on sin and a vindication of righteousness. When the fire of God fell on Elijah's altar, it was a fire of revival for the people, a vindication of God's spokesman, and a death sentence on the false prophets.

There is a principle here for understanding how revival works. If we restore the altar of the Lord as a place where real self-sacrifice can take place, and if we make that inner sacrifice in faith, God will meet us there. The fire of revival does not fall randomly or by accident here or there for no reason. The fire that comes from Heaven falls on the altar to consume the sacrificial offering. Jesus' death on the Cross is a clear picture of the sacrificial altar that God requires. When Jesus rose from the grave to sit at the Father's right hand, He then sent us the Holy Spirit. The fire of God subsequently fell on His disciples on the Day of Pentecost. This is the fire of revival that came to consume the sacrifice of their lives on the altar that Jesus had restored. It is time for the fire of the Holy Spirit to fall on us today, but first we must restore the altar of the Lord in Israel and throughout the nations.

We restore the altar of the Lord by gathering the living stones of God's scattered people. We are all just like the rough stones that Elijah found on the ground: we are just waiting to be used for something useful by God. The sacrifice that the Lord requires is restored when we make our own lives a meeting place for God. It is here that we can bring Him every weak and worthless thing—every idle and critical word, every selfish motive, every lustful thought, every cruel remark or deed, everything that is cowardly, every pain, affliction, and hurt. We must also bring to that altar every noble and good thing about us as an offering to God—our talents, our gifts, our future plans, our dreams. We bring them all to the Master as an irrevocable, non-returnable offering, and we let Him make of our entire lives what He desires—His good and perfect, eternal will. This is the place where true revival begins.

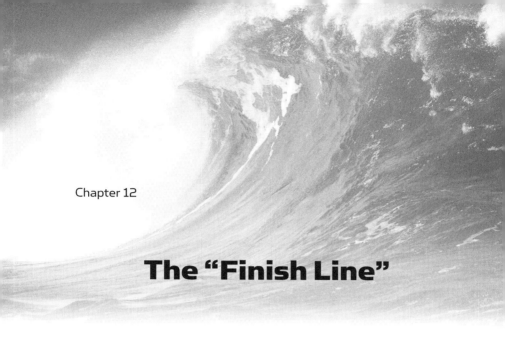

Chapter 12

The "Finish Line"

KEHILAT HACARMEL (Carmel Assembly) was founded on
Mount Carmel in 1991, and is the center of a "one new man"
(see Ephesians 2:15) community comprising Messianic Jews,
Arabs, and Gentiles from various nations. In 1996, ground was
broken for a new worship center near the highest point on
the Carmel ridge. The building was designed by a Messianic
Jewish architect, engineered by a Christian Arab, and built by
nearly five hundred volunteers from more than forty different
nations.

The foundations of the new building are built into the rock
of the mountain, and ten columns support the upper floors and
the roof. The rock of the mountain is like the Word of God in
Jesus' parable of the wise and foolish builders. (See Matthew
7:24.) The ten columns symbolize the Ten Commandments of
the law given by God to Moses. Four large arched windows
represent the four gospels of the New Testament. Our architect
said that he designed the structure of the building based on
God's covenant with Israel, with the windows letting in the
"light" of the gospels. In the center of the sanctuary is a circular
altar area with a large skylight directly above. Around the altar

are twelve rough stones that are placed there to remind us of the twelve stones Elijah used when he "repaired the altar of the Lord which had been torn down." (See I Kings 18:30-32.) The skylight represents an open heaven and the fire of God that fell upon Elijah's altar.

The walls of the semi-circular sanctuary are movable panels that allow additional seating outside on the balcony. The total seating comes to about eight hundred and fifty, which is meant to match the number Elijah's adversaries—four hundred and fifty prophets of Baal and four hundred prophets of the Asherah who ate at Jezebel's table. (See I Kings 18:19.) The Lord's commission to believers on the Carmel today is to train true prophets of God for His glory. The congregation's logo shows a mountain, the sea, and a small cloud. It is based on the Scripture from 1 Kings 18:44, where Elijah the prophet prayed for rain and told his servant seven times to go back and look for the rain cloud which he knew was coming. This means that intercessors must pray persistently, but revival on this mountain will surely come. Below the sanctuary level, there are classrooms and another smaller meeting area. Built into the foundation is a prayer "cave" dedicated to intercessory prayer for Israel and the nations. On the roof of the new building are two levels accessible by stairway for prayer walks in good weather. The Mediterranean Sea, Mount Tabor, Gilboa, and even Mount Hermon at the northernmost tip of Israel can be seen from the roof. Aside from serving as the home for our local congregation, the facility is used for teaching, worship, and intercessory prayer events that serve believers from various places in Israel and abroad. It is to be a *"house of prayer for all nations"* (Isaiah 56:7).

A building, which is the work of human hands, can do no more than point to the Creator and Lord of all. The people of God are His "living stones" (I Peter 2:5), and we ourselves are the temples of the Holy Spirit (see I Corinthians 3:16) where God himself dwells. Over the years, new congregations have been launched from this community on Mount Carmel. A Hebrew and Russian-speaking congregation is now thriving in Haifa's bay area. An outreach of humanitarian aid to Lebanese refugees in Israel resulted in the formation of a daughter congregation in Nahariya, a coastal city to the north. Recently, a new and fast growing Arabic-speaking congregation was planted in the downtown area of Haifa. In that vicinity, a clothing distribution facility mainly serving new immigrants is operating as well as "House of Victory," the drug and alcohol rehabilitation center where the congregation was born.

In response to an offer to view the film, *Jesus*, a depiction of the Gospel of Luke that has been produced in dozens of languages, many Russian-speaking Israelis began to visit the congregation. After decades of living under an oppressive Communist atheistic regime, they discovered that Jesus was truly the Messiah of the Jewish people, and their return to His land was indeed a prophetic fulfillment of the ancient Scriptures—not an event decided by politics. The commitment and joy in these new believers as they embrace faith in the God of Abraham, Isaac, and Jacob through Jesus has been tremendously exciting for our congregation and others throughout Israel. Every new expansion of God's Kingdom must face intense spiritual challenges to survive. As in the days when the children of Israel first entered this land, spiritual warfare is raging on Israel's high places. Mount Carmel's heritage is a prophetic confrontation between the Spirit of God and the demonic forces of idolatry. The prophet Isaiah foretold that the land of Israel would be spiritually desolate until God pours His Spirit upon the land from Heaven. The Hebrew word "Carmel" means a planted garden or field that is fertile and fruitful. In Isaiah's prophecy, "Carmel" is translated as "fruitful field." He wrote:

Until the Spirit is poured upon us from on high,
*and the wilderness becomes a **fruitful field** [Carmel],*

*and the **fruitful field** [Carmel] is counted as a forest*
(Isaiah 32:15).

In November 2002, the congregation of *Kehilat HaCarmel* took possession of two guesthouses located next to the congregational worship center. These facilities have been transformed into a center that functions as a place to nurture new ministries arising from our local congregation as well as those coming to Israel from other nations. It is a place for teaching and equipping the Lord's people that can also offer hospitality, prayer, and healing. Various ministries are being based at the center including discipleship training, counseling, and media development for outreach. A two-year, residential internship program called *Dor Elisha* (Elisha Generation) has been established as well as a refuge for women. The women's refuge serves Jewish, Arab, and other Gentile women in need of shelter, God's love, and spiritual oversight. Refugee women from Sudan and Eritrea with their children are among the residents. Various community services and humanitarian aid activities are utilizing the center. One of them is the "Raven's Basket" a program that provides food for Jewish, Druze, and Arab families in and around Haifa. Years ago, a "Prayer Summit" movement to bring congregational leaders in Haifa and throughout the Galilee together in prayer was launched in this facility. Now it will be used again to support this gathering and the renewal of local leadership through prayer.

The name for the new facility is *Or HaCarmel* or "Light of the Carmel." It takes its name and purpose from Isaiah's prophecy. *Or HaCarmel* is called to a dual role—to demonstrate the New Testament covenant of faith in the Messiah to the people of Israel, and to be a "light to the Gentiles" bringing revelation from God's word to the people of many nations.

I, the LORD, have called You in righteousness, and will hold Your hand; I will keep You and give You

*as a **covenant to the people, as a light to the Gentiles***
(Isaiah 42:6).

Headquartered at *Or HaCarmel* is the Mount Carmel
School of Ministry, an intensive, short-term training and tour
for Christians from the nations. The Mount Carmel School of
Ministry is for believers from any nation who want to acquire
a prophetic vision for the land and people of Israel. The school
has sessions several times each year. More information can be
found on the website: *www.mountcarmelsom.com*
The Scripture for the School of Ministry is found in the
first chapter of Luke.

*He will also go before Him **in the spirit and power of
Elijah**, "to turn the hearts of the fathers to the children,"
and the disobedient to the wisdom of the just, **to make
ready a people prepared for the Lord*** (Luke 1:17).

In 2005, *Kehilat HaCarmel* received the stewardship of
the *Beit Yedidia* (House of God's Friend) guest and conference
facility in Central Carmel. *Beit Yedidia* has become a community
center serving believing Jews and Arabs throughout the country.
As the Lord's ministries grow, we can see that the destiny of the
Carmel is in her name—fruitful and fertile for the Lord. God's
vision is to see His glory return to the Carmel and throughout
the land of Israel.

*The wilderness and the wasteland shall be glad for
them, and the desert shall rejoice and blossom as the
rose; it shall blossom abundantly and rejoice, even with
joy and singing. The glory of Lebanon shall be given
to it, **the excellence of Carmel** and Sharon. **They shall
see the glory of the LORD**, the excellency of our God*
(Isaiah 35:1-2).

Israel and the Nations

There is a prophetic connection between God's work on Mount Carmel and the great tsunami of revival in the nations. Micah wrote:

Shepherd Your people with Your staff, the flock of Your heritage, who dwell solitarily in a woodland, in the midst of Carmel; let them feed in Bashan and Gilead, as in days of old. As in the days when you came out of the land of Egypt, I will show them wonders. The nations shall see and be ashamed of all their might; they shall put their hand over their mouth; their ears shall be deaf (Micah 7:14-16).

Israel's destiny has always been intertwined with God's purposes for every other nation. In fact, the Bible states that God has established a relationship between the location of Israel and the inheritance of every other nation.

*When the Most High divided their inheritance to the nations, when He separated the sons of Adam, **He set the boundaries of the peoples according to the number of the children of Israel**. For the LORD's portion is His people; Jacob is the place of His inheritance* (Deuteronomy 32:8-9).

According to the Bible, Israel's portion of land on the Earth in some way influences the inheritance of every other nation. Therefore, it is a very serious matter for the nations to exert pressure on Israel to give up land to her enemies. In the book of the prophet Joel, God says that He will judge the nations that divide the land of Israel. Most people long for peace in the Middle East in order to end the terror and bloodshed. However, real peace is the result of changed hearts and not necessarily changed borders. There is great danger in trying to put a political band-aid on a deep spiritual wound. This is a biblical warning to political leaders of world powers in our day:

> *For behold, in those days and at that time, when I bring back the captives of Judah and Jerusalem, **I will also gather all nations, and bring them down to the Valley of Jehoshaphat; and I will enter into judgment with them there** on account of My people, My heritage Israel, whom they have scattered among the nations; they have also divided up My land* (Joel 3:1-2).

The "Finish Line"

Recently, I stood on the Mount of Olives in Jerusalem and gazed across the valley of the Kidron toward the Eastern Gate of the Old City. This is where the great tsunami of God's purposes throughout the nations will reach its conclusion. Here, the gospel began, the great prophets spoke, and King David set up his throne. It is here that Jesus died and rose from the dead and here the Lord will return at the end of history. Spiritual watchmen in Israel are prophetically holding up a banner to be seen by all believers in every nation. The banner reads, "Finish Line." Israel is prophetically positioned at the end of the long race to bring the gospel to the entire world, and at the end of the Jewish people's prolonged wandering among the nations. The massive currents of God's redemptive plans are converging on Israel and the city of Jerusalem. Who will catch the flow of these events and ride them toward their fulfillment? The turbulence of these final waves is daunting. The nation of Israel is destined to be a part of the rise and fall of many as we progress into the end-times.

The prophet Zechariah spoke of the end-times when he wrote:

> *Behold, **I will make Jerusalem a cup of drunkenness** to all the surrounding peoples, when they lay siege against*

Judah and Jerusalem. And it shall happen in that day that **I will make Jerusalem a very heavy stone for all peoples;** *all who would heave it away will surely be cut in pieces, though all nations of the earth are gathered against it* (Zechariah 12:2-3).

According to the prophet, the Spirit of the Lord will reach out to the Jewish people with the testimony of Jesus the Messiah. God will bring them to great repentance followed by national revival.

> *And I will pour on the house of David and on the inhabitants of Jerusalem the Spirit of grace and supplication; then* **they will look on Me whom they have pierced. Yes, they will mourn for Him as one mourns for his only son,** *and grieve for Him as one grieves for a firstborn* (Zechariah 12:10).

In the future, the nations will be drawn to Jerusalem, accepting God's choice of Israel and rejoicing together in the feast of the final harvest. Rain is essential for crops to survive and grow. It will be given to obedient nations that come to worship the God of Israel. In the Bible, rain is a symbol of the Holy Spirit, which is poured out by God in order to bring a rich spiritual harvest.

> *And it shall come to pass that everyone who is left of* **all the nations which came against Jerusalem shall go up from year to year to worship the King, the LORD of hosts, and to keep the Feast of Tabernacles.** *And it shall be that whichever of the families of the earth do not come up to Jerusalem to worship the King, the LORD of hosts, on them there will be no rain* (Zechariah 14:16-17).

The great end-time tsunami of God's purposes is more than worldwide revival. It is the power of God's presence sweeping through all the nations in order to fulfill His purposes, which were set in place before the world was made. The fulfillment of God's prophetic plans for Israel and the nations brings glory to Him among all the peoples of the world. When the tidal wave of God's purposes completes its circling of the globe and reaches its conclusion in Israel, the whole Earth will see the glory of God.

I bring My righteousness near, it shall not be far off; My salvation shall not linger. And I will place salvation in Zion, for Israel My glory (Isaiah 46:13).

For the earth will be filled with the knowledge of the glory of the LORD, as the waters cover the sea (Habakkuk 2:14).

Index